Electing Congress
The Financial Dilemma

Report of the Twentieth Century Fund Task Force
on Financing Congressional Campaigns

Background Paper by David L. Rosenbloom

The Twentieth Century Fund/New York/1970

SBN 87078-120-0
Copyright © 1970 by the Twentieth Century Fund, Inc.
Manufactured in the United States of America

Foreword

It is clear that there is something wrong with the nation's electoral system. There are many manifestations of popular disaffection. For example, there is the concern—expressed by politician and voter alike —with rising costs of campaigning, which suggests to some people that politics is an exclusive preserve of the rich and to others that it is a cynical and dirty business. The large number of votes recorded by a third party in the 1968 election is another sign of uneasiness. So, too, is the fact that many potential voters are staying away from the polls.

Both the Congress and the two major parties have been attempting to become more responsive to these and other signs of national concern. Congress is currently moving to eliminate or at least revise the Electoral College; at the same time, it is considering legislation to provide political candidates with greater access to television at less cost. Meanwhile, the major parties are seeking to carry out reforms that will enable them to attract people with ability and to open up their ranks to those—including many blacks, many poor, and many of the young—who now feel that the political system has nothing to offer them.

The Trustees of the Twentieth Century Fund, most of whom have been activist politically, have been no less concerned about the problems plaguing the political process in the United States. In 1967, the Fund sponsored the independent bipartisan Commission on Campaign Costs in the Electronic Era* to suggest reforms for campaigning on the presidential level. Its report, entitled *Voters' Time,* has served to stimulate debate and, hopefully, action, that will lead to better and cheaper exposure of presidential candidates on television as well as greater participation by the electorate in political campaigns.

The following report is an outgrowth of the deliberations of the Fund's Commission on Campaign Costs. For in reporting to the Fund, the Commission noted that the problems facing congressional candidates "may well be greater than those facing the national tickets." As one who was privileged to sit in on some of the meetings of the Commission, I can attest to its own concern about the difficulties of entry into politics for people who are not rich or well-connected and its feeling that new ways must be found to broaden and expand public participation in the political system.

As a result, the Trustees last year approved the setting up of a Fund Task Force to specifically consider the problems of congressional campaign financing. We were fortunate in assembling a distinguished and ecumenical group who, collectively, possessed an extraordinary amount of experience and information about political campaigns at the congressional level. Moreover, it was a deeply committed Task Force, one that was not only aware of the multiple problems involved in congressional campaigning but determined to do something constructive about them.

Like most other Fund Task Forces, the report of the Task Force is accompanied by a background paper that provides details and outlines the dimensions of the problems under discussion. It was prepared by David Rosenbloom, of the Political Science Department of M.I.T., who also served as the Task Force's rapporteur.

The Task Force demonstrated its commitment in its willingness to devote time and energy to the assignment. It held spirited debates on many issues but, partly because of the display of cooperative zeal on the part of Thomas B. Curtis, the Task Force chairman and a former Republican Congressman, and Neil Staebler, its vice chairman and a former Democratic Congressman, and partly because the group as

---

*Newton N. Minow, Chairman; Dean Burch; Thomas G. Corcoran; Alexander Heard; Robert Price.

iv

a whole believed that the problems required consensus solutions, there were very few instances where the Task Force could not come to unanimous agreement on the proposals for reform. Yet their all but unanimous recommendations are not watered down compromises. In almost every case, they involve very real reforms of our electoral processes.

The Fund, its Trustees, and its staff appreciate the efforts made by the Task Force to produce a provocative, timely and useful report. In this congressional campaign year, the nation's political system will undergo new pressures and strains. It is our belief that the Task Force report offers positive remedies for many of the ills of the system.

M. J. Rossant
April 1970

Contents

Members of the Task Force

Herbert E. Alexander
Director
Citizens' Research Foundation

Charles Barr
Administrative Assistant to the Chairman of the Board
Standard Oil Company (Indiana)

Thomas B. Curtis, *Chairman*
Former Congressman
St. Louis, Missouri

Russell D. Hemenway
Director
National Committee for an Effective Congress

David Jones
Executive Vice President
Charles Edison Youth Fund

Vernon E. Jordan, Jr.
Director
United Negro College Fund, Inc.

John P. Sears
Campaign Consultant
Lexington, Massachusetts

Neil Staebler, *Vice Chairman*
Former Congressman and Democratic National Committeeman
from Michigan

Mary Zon
Research Director
Committee for Political Education, AFL-CIO

Rapporteur: David L. Rosenbloom

REPORT OF THE TASK FORCE

Report of the Task Force

The hoped-for objective of this report is simple: a fair, competitive election for every seat in the United States Congress. This objective requires that a candidate have access to adequate resources to wage a competitive campaign. We believe also that campaigns should be financed in a way that will build support for our political institutions and respect for the political process.

There will always be some imbalance between candidates in an election. One candidate will have advantages—well-known image, issues, or events—over another. These advantages obviously cannot be eliminated. However, the imbalance of money and other campaign resources which now prevents many elections from being competitive, can be reduced.

At present, about 25 per cent of the elections to Congress represent serious competition, that is, instances where the decision rests on less than a 60–40 per cent split of vote. An overwhelming proportion of elections are won by incumbents. (See charts 1 and 2.) Since 1954 incumbents have been involved in 3,220 House and 224 Senate primary or general elections. They have won 92 per cent and 85 per cent of them, respectively. (See charts 3 and 4.)

The growing success of these incumbents at the polls is closely related to current patterns of congressional campaign finance. In-

CHART 1

INCUMBENCY IN THE U.S. SENATE

MEAN LENGTH OF SERVICE OF SENATORS

NEW MEMBERS ELECTED TO THE SENATE

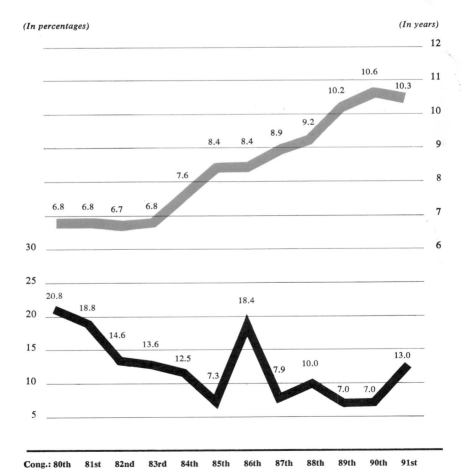

(In percentages)   *(In years)*

Cong.: 80th   81st   82nd   83rd   84th   85th   86th   87th   88th   89th   90th   91st

CHART 2

INCUMBENCY IN THE HOUSE OF REPRESENTATIVES

MEAN LENGTH OF SERVICE OF REPRESENTATIVES

NEW MEMBERS ELECTED TO THE HOUSE

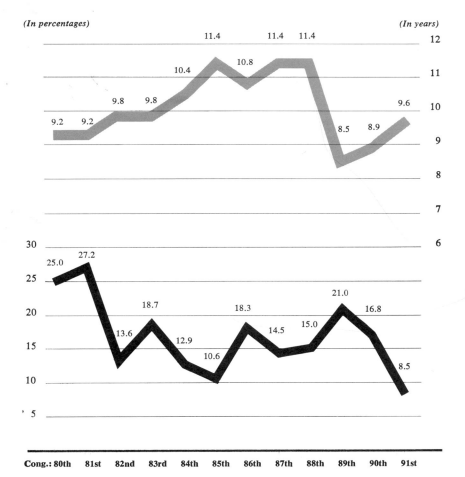

CHART 3

SENATORS RUNNING FOR RE-ELECTION IN
PRIMARY OR GENERAL ELECTIONS, 1954-1968

TOTAL INVOLVED

TOTAL RE-ELECTED

TOTAL DEFEATED

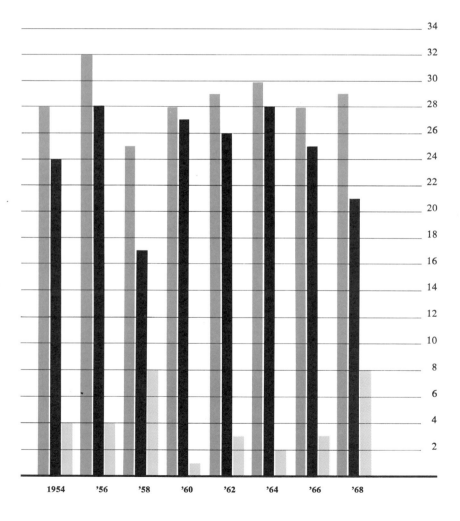

CHART 4

**REPRESENTATIVES RUNNING FOR RE-ELECTION IN
PRIMARY OR GENERAL ELECTIONS, 1954-1968**

TOTAL INVOLVED

TOTAL RE-ELECTED

TOTAL DEFEATED

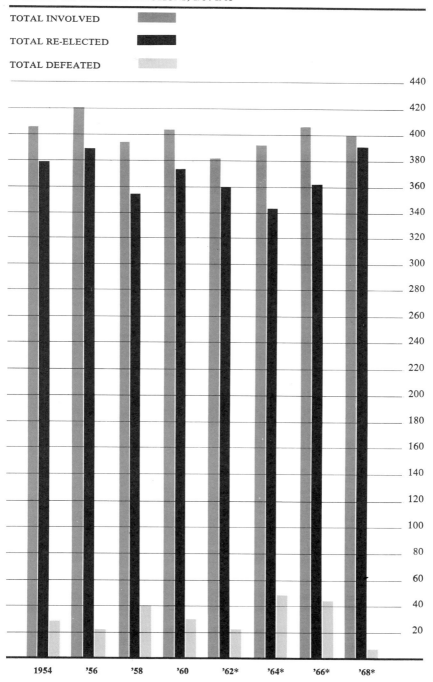

*The 1962, '64, '66, and '68 elections were affected by constant redistricting in the states. These figures do not include instances in which incumbents were forced to run against incumbents either in a primary or general because of redistricting.
In 1962 there were 12 such cases, 3 in 1964, 3 in 1966 and 5 in 1968.

ıts start a campaign well ahead of the challengers and usually
head. Incumbency in Congress gives a person access to cam-
ı resources that make his re-election highly probable. The incumbent has the natural advantages of experience, previous public
exposure, and a public record. Additionally he has the perquisites of
office—especially his staff, his offices, his almost unlimited free postage—to help his re-election campaign.

The incumbent also has easy access to large special interest contributors* and to the national party campaign committees. Many
incumbents begin their re-election campaigns with major portions of
their funds already collected or pledged from Washington-based
special interest groups. Some incumbents, especially those holding
important committee assignments, can mobilize allies in the federal
bureaucracy to help their re-election. Federal departments and agencies can grant or withhold federal contracts, appointments, or other
redeemable political favors.

Many incumbents benefit in still another way. In setting House
district boundaries, state legislatures often try to protect the incumbents in order to increase the seniority of their state's congressional
delegation.

It is no accident that incumbents win so often. Many congressional elections are over before they begin because the challengers
simply cannot raise the resources they need to overcome the advantages of the incumbents.

The cost of an effective campaign for Congress is rising rapidly.
Today a competitive campaign for a House seat can cost each side
more than $100,000, while a Senate contest can cost each campaigner
a minimum of $250,000 even in a relatively small state.

With the exception of incumbents in "safe" districts, successful
candidates for Congress must either be wealthy or have access to
large sums of money. Challengers without such resources do run for
Congress. Most lose.

The rapid rise in cost can be traced largely to changing communication patterns in the country. Most Senate campaigns and many
House campaigns make heavy investments in television and radio
time. In 1966 expenditures for all electoral advertising time on tele-

*We define a special interest contributor as any individual or association that has limited
objectives in politics and makes contributions to promote them.

vision and radio were $32 million, about 1½ times what was spent in 1962. A substantial portion of this total was spent on congressional campaigns. If the laws are not changed, more than $50 million will be spent in 1970.

Direct mail has long been used by congressional candidates to communicate with the voters. In recent years, however, it has become much more expensive. The cost of first-class postage has doubled since 1958 and will increase in 1970. In addition, the advent of computerized mailing techniques has made the use of direct mail both more effective and more costly.

The easy availability of air transportation is enabling more candidates to travel more. Despite the growth of mass media communication, candidates for Congress are making more personal appearances at greater cost to their campaigns than was true in the past. Some of this travel, in fact, is designed to create events for free publicity on news and interview shows.

To make full use of modern communications techniques candidates for Congress are turning increasingly to professional pollsters, managers, public relations firms, and advertising companies. These professionals often help candidates, but they also add to the cost of a campaign.

Despite the new ways of reaching the electorate, too many elections remain uncompetitive because a significant number of Americans do not vote. In 1970 less than half of the eligible population will vote in the congressional elections.* While the total number of people participating in congressional elections has grown in the last twenty years there has been no substantial change in the proportion of the eligible population that actually participates in congressional elections. (See chart 5.)

Many Americans are still prevented from voting. Economic and social repression has left many black, poor, and uneducated citizens afraid or unable to vote. Candidates who try to make their campaigns competitive by registering and involving groups that have been denied the ballot have found the process expensive and frustrating.

Lengthy residence requirements are still commonly used by some

*We define eligible population as all those citizens who have reached voting age. We use this base because we believe that everyone who has reached voting age should be registered to vote. Voting participation figures would be even lower if the two million Americans outside the country were included.

political organizations to keep voter turnout low and relatively controlled. Many Americans whose occupations force them to move frequently are in fact disenfranchised. Others who are away from their homes on election day are disenfranchised because absentee ballot provisions in many states are complicated and make voting difficult. Others do not vote because of indifference to the particular candidates or to the political system itself.

Voter frauds in some areas keep campaigns uncompetitive. Votes cast go uncounted, votes may be bought, and fictitious votes may be recorded. Overcoming or eliminating these frauds is also expensive and frustrating.

Large amounts of money and other resources are now raised and spent, but not nearly as much as would need to be spent if all congressional elections were competitive. We must invest more money more wisely, to balance the advantages of incumbents, to finance adequate access to contemporary communications, to bring many excluded citizens into the electoral process, and to bring back those alienated from it.

To achieve the objective of fair competitive congressional elections changes must be made in the public policies which regulate the conduct and distribution of resources to congressional campaigns.

CHART 5

VOTER PARTICIPATION IN CONGRESSIONAL ELECTIONS, 1930–1968

PRESIDENTIAL YEARS

NON-PRESIDENTIAL YEARS

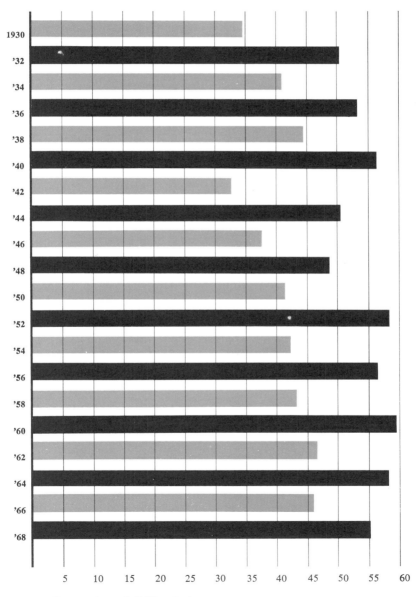

(In percentages of eligible voters)

SOURCE: *Congress and the Nation,* Vol. II,
Congressional Quarterly, Washington, D.C., 1969, p. 439.

RECOMMENDATIONS

I. Publicizing Campaign Finance

1. Full Disclosure

We believe that full public disclosure and publication of all campaign contributions and expenditures are the best disciplines available to make campaigns honest and fair. We also believe full public reporting will tell the public where political contributions are going, where they are needed, and thus encourage more people to make contributions to political campaigns.

More than half the money spent in congressional elections today is not reported to the public. The federal Corrupt Practices Act requires candidates and committees to file reports on contributions and expenditures, but the law is riddled with loopholes and, as a result, few campaigns are fully reported. In 1968, 182 candidates for Congress filed reports stating that they had personally spent nothing and knew of no committee expenditures that needed to be reported at the federal level.

Some of those who reported nothing at the federal level filed more complete campaign income and spending reports with state or county agencies. However, thirty-one states either have no reporting laws or require reports of varying degrees of completeness only after an election. Almost no state has adequate auditing or enforcement procedures to deter or uncover illegal activities. As a result of the weaknesses of federal and state laws, some candidates spend more than $1 million in their campaigns without reporting any of it to the public.

Total spending on the 1968 congressional campaigns reported under the federal statutes totaled $8,482,857. Actual spending was probably more than $50 million. We believe the public has the right to know who is paying how much for congressional campaigns. So long as the public is denied this information, beliefs about political finance that undermine respect for our political institutions will persist. The routine failure of candidates for high public office to disclose how much they spent in their campaigns and where they got the money contributes to this growing cynicism. If respect for our political institutions is to be restored, finance regulations must be changed. The public cannot be expected to respect the law when those who would be its lawmakers avoid or break the law to get elected.

Information about campaign finance should be available to the public in easily comprehended form *during* the campaign. Both the public and the candidates should be confident that attempts to conceal campaign contributions or expenditures will be investigated, exposed, and penalized.

At present, the federal statute specifically excludes primary elections from reporting requirements. In many areas primaries are more important than general elections. We believe that money contributed and spent to influence the selection of the party nominees in a federal election should be as fully reported to the public as the contributions and expenditures of the election itself.

We recommend that every political organization and committee that spends money or other resources to influence a primary or general election for federal office be required to register with a federal elections commission and to keep orderly and open records of its activities.

Any such organization or committee that raises or spends $1,000 or more in any year should be required to file a report with a federal elections commission quarterly and fifteen and five days prior to a primary or general election.

Reports should be clear, simple, and easy for the public to understand. They should provide complete information about the source of all contributions, pledges, and new or outstanding loans; and about the recipient and purpose of all expenditures.

We recommend that firm and realistic penalties be established and enforced to deter late, inaccurate, or incomplete reports. Candidates and their authorized agents should be held responsible for the accuracy and completeness of reports filed by their campaign committees.

2. Federal Elections Commission

No agency is now responsible for supervising compliance with federal campaign finance regulations. The Secretary of the Senate and the Clerk of the House are the statutory repositories for campaign spending reports but they do not have the authority, the staff, or the motivation to do anything but accept the reports that are filed. Further, there is no office that keeps records and provides information about political contributions and expenditures of committees seeking to influence federal elections.

There is no federal agency that regularly investigates serious charges of illegal conduct during a campaign. Nor is there any agency competent to give legal advice about campaign activities. We believe this administrative void must be filled if campaign finance regulations are to be effective.

We recommend the establishment of a bipartisan federal elections commission to administer regulations affecting federal campaigns. The commission should audit and publicize all campaign finance reports and report possible violations, including late filing, to the appropriate enforcement agencies for action. The commission should have the staff, resources, and independence to do the jobs assigned to it. It should have the power to investigate charges of illegal activity in federal campaigns, to subpoena evidence, and to establish uniform accounting and reporting procedures for political committees.

3. Spending Limits

The traditional intent of campaign finance regulation in the United States has been to limit the size of campaign contributions and expenditures and to prohibit contributions from certain sources. The Corrupt Practices Act limits the amounts candidates and political committees may spend in any one year and limits the contributions an individual may make to a political committee in any year.

Contributions from corporations, unions, and government contractors are prohibited entirely.

We do not believe this policy of ceilings has served the public well because expenditures have been neither limited nor disclosed. The limits now in the law—$5,000 for a House candidate, $25,000 for a Senate candidate, and $3 million a year for a political committee —are unrealistically low. They do not significantly affect the amount of campaign spending. They are unenforceable and while some members of the Task Force would prefer legal limits we believe that no workable set of limits can be devised.

Many people are concerned that candidates spend too much in their campaigns. At least one candidate for the House in 1968 spent $2 million in the general election alone. In some Senate campaigns, in the primary and general elections, as much as $5 or $6 million have been spent. Current laws have been ineffective in preventing or disclosing these expenditures.

If there were full public disclosure and publication of all campaign contributions and expenditures during a campaign, the voters themselves could better judge whether a candidate has spent too much. This policy would do more to protect the political system from unbridled spending than legal limits on the size of contributions and expenditures.

Some candidates probably spend too much, but that is not the point; the larger problem is that many candidates, especially challengers, do not have enough money for their election campaigns. **We recommend that all spending limits for congressional campaigns be eliminated.**

4. Limits on Individual Contributions

This Task Force was concerned that removing all limits on individual contributions to political committees might open the prospect of rich individuals buying federal elections. We would like to protect our political system from that threat. The Task Force agreed that neither rich candidates spending their own money, nor rich contributors supporting a candidate should be allowed to have undue influence on elections. Full disclosure will warn the voters when such an attempt is being made.

The Corrupt Practices Act prohibits individuals from giving more than $5,000 to a political committee in any year. This law has not deterred people who wanted to make large contributions to candidates. They simply give their contributions to several committees supporting the same candidate.

Gifts, including political contributions, of more than $3,000 to any single recipient in any year are subject to the gift tax provisions of the internal revenue code. This may be a more effective restraint on individual contributions than the limit in the Corrupt Practices Act.

Several members of the Task Force favor a limit on the amount an individual, including the candidate himself, may contribute to a campaign. Mary Zon and Thomas B. Curtis believe that such a limit should be enacted and can be enforced. However, we were unable to prescribe an effective device for enforcing such a recommendation.

We considered recommending a $5,000 limit on individual contributions even though it might not be fully enforceable. But since we believe one of the principal challenges of our electoral system is to restore its credibility with large numbers of the American people, we were reluctant to recommend anything that we did not think could be enforced. Moreover, we feel that unreported large contributions are much more of a danger than large contributions that are publicly reported.

The principal burden for reporting campaign contributions and expenditures ought to be borne by campaign organizations. However, reports from individuals who contribute substantial amounts of money to politics will serve as a valuable addition and cross-check to these reports.

We recommend that limits on the size of individual contributions to political committees be eliminated.

We recommend that individuals who contribute more than $5,000 in a year to federal candidates and political committees be required to file a report with a federal elections commission listing the date, recipient, and amount of all contributions (including purchases of tickets to fund-raising events), pledges and loans of $100 or more, and the aggregate total of all contributions of less than $100. Such donors should be required to certify that they have contributed their own money and that they will not be reimbursed in any way.

5. Ban on Contributions from Corporations, Unions, Trade Associations, and Government Contractors

Corporations, unions, and government contractors are now prohibited from making contributions to federal campaigns. Several ways have been developed to evade this prohibition. In the past, however, there have been only sporadic efforts to enforce this ban.

But we believe that corporations, unions, trade associations, and government contractors are unacceptable as sources of money and resources for federal campaigns. Contributions from these sources create too many potential, ethical problems for both the contributors and the recipients. We believe candidates should guard against such contributions. When illegal contributions are discovered and prosecuted, the names of the candidates who received them should be released to the public. This has not happened in the recent prosecutions.

Mary Zon objects to the equating of unions and corporations because of their wholly different purpose, constituencies, and methods of adopting and administering policies are different.

We recommend corporate and union nonpartisan efforts to encourage employees and members to contribute personal money and time to political campaigns and parties. We encourage corporations and unions to expand these activities. They should be allowed to continue financing them with regular operating funds.

We recommend that current prohibitions against corporate, union, and government contractor contributions to federal campaigns be continued and vigorously enforced. When a corporation, union, association, or contractor is prosecuted for making illegal contributions to federal campaigns the names of candidates who received such contributions should be released to the public.

We recommend that nonpartisan political solicitation programs financed by corporate and union operating funds be encouraged.

6. A Single Responsible Campaign Committee

A common way for candidates and their managers to avoid the current limitations on spending and reporting is to establish many committees to finance and organize a single campaign. This procedure usually obscures information about the amount and sources of money spent in their campaigns. We believe that the elimination of contributing and spending limits removes any possible justification for the establishment of multiple financial structures for any congressional election campaign. To simplify disclosure of the sources of funds and use of money being spent in any campaign, only one official campaign committee should be established.

The majority of the task force members believe that if this recommendation is to be effective, individual contributors should make all of their contributions to one committee. Neil Staebler and Charles Barr are concerned that limiting individuals in this manner is impractical and may, in fact, have an adverse effect on broadening the base of campaign givers.

We know that many candidates and managers believe it is useful to organize their campaigns around many specialized committees. We have no intention of interfering with the proliferation of political committees unless this practice is carried out to evade the law and obscure financial data. This recommendation would not stop truly independent committees supporting a candidate from being set up.

We recommend that all candidates for federal office be required to designate one official campaign committee. All subsidiary and specialized committees should be responsible to the official campaign committee which shall file all required income and spending reports for the entire campaign. Individuals should be prohibited from making contributions to more than one committee organized specifically to support the same candidate.

II. Increasing Participation

7. Tax Credit for Individual Contributions

We believe the best political finance system would be one based on relatively small contributions from large numbers of citizens. The number of small givers (under $100), especially to the Republican party, has been growing substantially. We think this desirable trend should be encouraged.

A modest tax credit for small political contributors probably will increase their number for two reasons. For one thing, the availability of the credit itself will enable many more people to afford a small contribution. For another, a government tax credit will make political contributions more respectable. Many people are still reluctant to contribute to politics because they think there is something "wrong" with political finance.

Only about 8 per cent of Americans said they had made political contributions in 1968. Polls indicate, however, that many more would have given if they had been asked. We believe that a tax credit will create an opportunity for candidates and parties to raise more money in small amounts, provided they do a better job of solicitation. We urge the parties to cooperate with other institutions in the society to train more competent party officials and workers.

We have recommended a tax credit rather than a deduction because deductions favor higher bracket taxpayers. Our approach builds in the element of personal involvement, by allowing a credit for only part of the contributions.

We recommend a tax credit of up to $25 ($50 on a joint return) for 50 per cent of contributions made during a year to political committees.

8. Full Voter Registration

While some improvement has been made in removing impediments to voting, we believe the nation must take a much more positive approach to insure that every citizen who reaches voting age is registered to vote. We believe national voter registration financed by the federal government would strengthen our democratic system and remove this financial burden from individual candidates, parties, and other private organizations.

We recommend that the Congress establish a simple and universal pattern for complete voter registration, including citizens who are abroad. This should be carried out through a new unit in one of the federal agencies or through subsidies to states that adopt model uniform legislation for this purpose.

9. Voters' Information

We believe voter participation and electoral competition would be increased if all voters were given full information about the electoral process, such as the hours and places of voting and use of the absentee ballot.

We believe this should be provided at public expense. Some states already mail such information to their voters about the election procedures and the candidates and issues on the ballot. This practice should be expanded so that each voter receives official information about the election and his voting rights. We feel the states are best able to gather and distribute this information to the voters. This activity should be supported by postal subsidies.

We recommend that the federal government provide postage for voters' information material prepared by each state. To be eligible for free postage such material should include facts about voters' rights and the federal elections on the ballot.

10. Postal Privileges for National Party Committees

We believe a slight change in federal policy would encourage our political parties to communicate with their members more frequently. With regular communication they could recruit new people as volunteers and donors. Regular political communication from the parties might ease the financial and physical burdens congressional candidates now face every two years in searching out and activating their party's members. Further, reduced postage would encourage parties to expand direct mail solicitation of small gifts.

We recommend that national committees of political parties (defined as having had congressional candidates in one-half of the states in the most recent or current congressional election) be allowed to use the lowest postal rate available to charitable organizations.

III. Increasing Competition

11. Use of Congressional Facilities

A better balance of resources between incumbents and challengers would produce genuinely competitive contests for the Congress. One means which we considered for correcting this imbalance is full cash subsidies for political campaigns.

We decided not to recommend this approach because we think it could lead to less political participation. Broad-based fund raising by political parties and candidates is a more effective way to achieve greater participation. Furthermore, if candidates got money directly from the government the parties might be even weaker than they are now, and their ability to organize government might erode even more. On the other hand, if parties alone got the government subsidies, their power would increase inordinately and the balance between a candidate's independence and his party loyalty would be threatened.

Our objective of more competitive elections can be accomplished through new federal policies that would prevent incumbents from using their public office for campaign purposes and which would ease the financial burden on all candidates for Congress. Many members now use their congressional offices to plan and conduct their re-election campaigns. Congressional staff members often spend significant amounts of time working on the next election. Hometown offices of members of Congress sometimes serve as campaign headquarters.

Members of Congress often use the extensive radio and television recording facilities in the Capitol to tape politically oriented messages for broadcast in their campaigns. The postal franking privilege has at times been abused for political mailings.

Members of Congress are entitled to ask staff people to work on campaigns. But we believe these people should leave the federal payroll during the campaign and be paid by the campaign organization. This would put the incumbent on an equal footing with the challenger who must pay his staff from campaign funds. Similarly, incumbents should not be allowed to use government facilities and equipment to plan and organize their campaigns. They should maintain separate campaign facilities paid for by their campaign organization.

We recommend that a federal elections commission enforce rules that will prevent members of Congress from using their staff, office, and communications facilities to plan and run their re-election campaigns.

12. Postal Allowance for Candidates

It would be relatively cheap for the federal government to give each candidate for Congress the opportunity to put a piece of his own literature into the hands of each voter. While we are dealing here only with the general election we realize that in some areas the primary is still the most important arena in an electoral competition. If our recommendation proves to be as useful as we think it will, it could easily be extended to candidates in primary elections.

We recommend that every legally qualified candidate for Congress in the general election be entitled to one free mail delivery to each voter in his constituency.

13. Access to Television and Radio

The Federal Communications Act of 1934 authorizes licenses to use but not to own the airwaves. We believe the airwaves belong to the people. We believe it to be proper public policy to assure candidates for federal office the right to use television and radio to communicate with their constituents during an election.

To implement this policy, legally qualified candidates must be granted reasonable requests to buy television and radio time. Some broadcasters refuse all political candidates the right to buy time.

David Jones recommends that broadcasters be prohibited from denying a legally qualified candidate any reasonable request for time he may wish to purchase in general or primary elections. He opposes mandating that broadcasters sell time at discounted prices. The other Task Force members believe that broadcasters should be required to sell time at reduced prices to provide access to television and radio to candidates of modest means.

In metropolitan areas television and radio stations encompass several House districts. In these areas television and radio are not effective campaign tools, at any price, and we do not encourage candidates to use them. We are therefore against mandating free time for *all* congressional candidates. We have limited ourselves to the problem of assuring candidates access to television advertising and political programming at reasonable prices. We believe more intensive study of the political uses of television is needed to insure that this important public resource is used to increase the quality of public knowledge and debate on important issues. For example, we think there should be much more comparative examination of the uses, impact, and effects of various formats as political communication tools.

The study of presidential television campaigning conducted by the Twentieth Century Fund Commission on Campaign Costs in the Electronic Era *(Voters' Time)* was useful. We urge that new studies of the impact and effects of television at all levels of the political system be conducted.

We recommend that commercial broadcasters be required to sell reasonable amounts of prime and other time to legally qualified candidates for Congress.

We recommend that commercial broadcasters be required to charge all legally qualified candidates for Congress for such political time as they buy in general and primary elections at no more than 50 per cent of the lowest charge made to any commercial advertiser for such time, provided that broadcasters may then, for federal income tax purposes, deduct amounts equal to the dollar value of such discounts to candidates from their total taxable income.

14. Potential of Cable Television

Multichannel cable television is coming into wide use throughout the country. Because cable television is highly flexible and can deliver programs to limited geographic areas such as congressional districts, ground rules for the design and use of cable television systems ought to provide for effective use of this medium for political communication.

We recommend that in formulating regulations for the use of multichannel cable television, the F.C.C. take due regard of the tremendous political value cable television will provide in campaigns within limited geographical constituencies. Regulations governing the use of cable television should allow for maximum use of these facilities for political communication.

IV. Organizing Reform

15. A Select Committee of Congress

Under current congressional procedures recommendations for improving the system of congressional campaign finance fall under the jurisdiction of several different committees. We believe prospects for comprehensive examination and reform of our campaign finance procedures will be improved if one committee of the Congress has the authority to examine all of the important regulatory, financial, and communications aspects of federal election campaigns.

We recommend that a select committee of the Congress be appointed to study and recommend legislation that will improve congressional campaign finance practices.

16. An Investigating Committee for the 1970 Congressional Elections

If past reporting practice is any indication of what will happen in 1970, the public will not be provided with adequate information about the financing of congressional campaigns. If changes in reporting are not made between now and the elections, more than half the money spent will go unreported. Even if a thorough study is made afterward, much information about campaign practices will remain unknown because campaign organizations and records often disperse quickly after the election.

We recommend that a special investigating subcommittee be in operation throughout the 1970 congressional election campaigns to gather information about the financing of campaigns while they are taking place. The subcommittee should make information about the sources and uses of campaign funds available to the public.

BACKGROUND PAPER
by David L. Rosenbloom

Author's Preface

While the background paper reflects things I have learned from members of the Task Force, the views and possible errors in it are my own. I accept full responsibility for them. I want to thank all the members of the Task Force for their help and suggestions. I am grateful to Herbert Alexander for making the facilities of the Citizens' Research Foundation and his own considerable knowledge available to me.

Only the quick mind, wit and fingers of my secretary for this project, Nancy Rich, made it possible to come close to our deadline. I also owe a debt of gratitude to Alan Tipermas, my research assistant, for his work, to Stanley H. Brown, who applied his excellent editing skills to improve the paper, and to Frederick H. Sontag for his continuing concern and suggestions.

Finally, I want to thank the Director and the Board of Trustees of the Twentieth Century Fund for entrusting the staffwork to a team of young people. It is our generation that will suffer longest if congressional campaigns and the public policies enacted by the winners are not made more democratic and responsive.

I. Congressional Campaign Finance

As this year's congressional elections approach, almost to a man candidates will avoid, circumvent, and occasionally evade just about all the laws of the states and the national government that regulate the political fund-raising process. Secret conduits, spurious committees, and other forms of deceit and subterfuge will come into existence to provide the candidates with the money they need to reach voters. Men of good will, with the best intentions, will take money from sources that are proscribed against giving it; it will come in prohibited quantities; and much, if not most, will go unreported and even unrecorded. In addition, the ability of incumbents to retain their seats (see charts 1–4) indicates strongly that their challengers often cannot get enough money to finance effective campaigns. That makes the very process of democratic representation an exercise in both futility and hypocrisy.

The flouting of the law that has apparently become a political necessity, while deplorable in itself, creates by-products even more pernicious. No single element of the electoral system contributes so emphatically to making politics a dirty word in the American lexicon. Moreover, to finance their increasingly costly campaigns, candidates frequently rely on a few large contributions from individuals or special interest groups. When they take their seats, then, they are representing not only their explicit constituencies but also a sort of shadow constituency of large donors.

If otherwise law-abiding men must ignore laws to engage in congressional politics, the fault must lie somewhere among the state and federal statutes that purport to render elections sanitary. For they obviously do not succeed.

The controls on election finance function so poorly for several reasons: archaic statutes persist through an inertial force of their own; others persist because they offer short-run advantages to those who have the power to change them; and lawmakers have been reluctant to call attention to widespread abuses for fear public cynicism would mount and reflect on them. Until recently, they have acted only in the wake of scandals.

The recommendations of the Task Force were developed against a context that included the structure of Congress and congressional elections, the history of political finance regulation, current campaign finance practices, present legislation, and recent proposals for changing campaign finance. All these elements will be examined here in terms of their contributions to the objectives of the American system of representative government.

Obviously the primary over-all objective must be to reinforce the ability of the system to function effectively by encouraging the best people to participate regardless of their wealth or connections. Candidates must have reasonable access to sufficient funds and resources so that they can compete effectively and represent their constituents without undue encumbrance or obligation. To achieve this, the political system must work to produce genuinely competitive elections for every seat in Congress. It must provide the electorate with enough information about the sources and amounts of campaign funds so that the voters will have a clear understanding of whom else, besides themselves, their Representatives and Senators represent and where they can fix responsibility for their actions.

It must also provide a better balance between incumbents and challengers. Though incumbents have natural advantages over challengers simply because they are Representatives and Senators rather than aspirants, incumbency also produces potent financial benefits. Officeholders have paid staffs and offices, free use of the mail, and frequent access to their constituents through the news media. These perquisites probably give the incumbents a financial advantage over their challengers worth a minimum of $16,000 per election. This rough and probably very low estimate includes $6,000 for congressional staff time used for campaigns, $2,400 for government offices and facilities used, $7,200 for campaign material mailed under the frank,[1] and $2,500 that incumbents can forgo and challengers need for minimal name exposure on billboards to offset the recognition that inheres in an incumbent by virtue of his position. In general, they also have greater access to campaign contributions from national political organizations than their competitors. The congressional campaign committees of both parties give most of their money and resources to incumbents, the principal exception being the Republican Congressional Booster Club, which gives only to challengers. Special interest groups such as corporations, trade and regional associations, and labor unions also favor incumbents, because they know where they stand on their special interests.

With so much going for them, it is not surprising that incumbents rarely lose. If challengers were able to raise sufficient funds to offset the advantages of incumbents, the total cost of electing a House and a Senate would probably cost far more than it does today, not only because of the size of the differential but also because reaching voters is an increasingly expensive job.

Current regulations of campaign finance, according to former President Lyndon B. Johnson, are more loophole than law.[2] Their principal effect seems to be to force candidates and political managers to lie or to conceal their fund-raising activities, even when no other ethical consideration than the regulatory requirements is at stake. Getting elected simply takes more money than the laws provide for.[3]

Many of the myths about little black satchels full of money and dirty politics have developed because there is little hard information about political finance. Questionable practices exacerbate the problem of fixing responsibility on candidates for their actions and promises during campaigns. It takes a lot of people and activities to run a political campaign, and the problem of assigning responsibility for these people and their actions is difficult at best. But when the electorate is excluded from substantial knowledge about money and sources, it is also excluded from the ability to assign true responsibility. That becomes even more significant when the candidate who cannot be held responsible for his campaign becomes a member of Congress. The problem is not merely one of recording, reporting, and publicity but timing as well. After elections, hot issues cool.

With considerations such as these in mind, the following survey of campaign finance regulation has been made. It does not pretend to be exhaustive. Rather, its purpose has been relevance to the realities of politics and the obvious need for change in the system of financing campaigns.

II. Special Problems of Congressional Campaigns

Congressional elections differ from others because of the structure of the Congress itself and because of the place of Congress in the spectrum of the American political system. More money is spent on congressional elections than on presidential elections. And while in the twentieth century presidential elections have usually been extremely competitive, congressional elections, especially in the House, have not. Frequent turnover of the presidency is now assured by the constitutional two-term limit. But in Congress the benefits of the seniority system and the natural desire for job security make longevity in office an important goal for almost every member. Incumbency can be an electoral advantage only once for a President. But for Congressmen and Senators the advantages of incumbency are cumulative.[4]

Congressional elections are also affected by the constitutional division and separation of powers. Each state legislature is charged with the primary responsibility for establishing equitable district boundaries for its members in the House of Representatives. In recent years, the federal courts, as a result of the United States Supreme Court's one-man-one-vote doctrine, have been able to order many states to redraw their boundaries to make them equal in population or more compact and contiguous.

Drawing congressional district boundaries is a high-level political art form. In almost any state, it is possible to draw several different sets of boundaries which could meet court tests of equality yet produce wide variations in election results. By making marginal adjustments in borders, state legislatures often can create districts that are safe for one party. The majority party in a state legislature generally tries to gain partisan advantage for itself while protecting incumbents by assuring them safe districts.[5]

The public supervision of congressional elections is complicated by the fact that both state and federal laws operate. The Constitution allows the states the prerogative of determining the time and manner of elections, but reserves to the federal government the right to intervene.[6]

The place of the Congress in the political system creates other differences between congressional and other types of elections. House districts do not necessarily follow the county lines traditionally used by political parties for their organizational boundaries. As a result, a candidate for the House often must build his own political organization.

Since a Senator's term is six years, his campaign may or may not coincide with a gubernatorial or other election contest. Senate candidates, therefore, often must also build their own campaign organizations. But a Senator can run for another office, Governor or President, without resigning or even risking his seat. He also may face competition from state officers with four-year terms who can run against him in the middle of their terms without giving up their offices.

The national committees of the political parties are primarily concerned with presidential elections. There is often tension and competition for funds between the congressional campaign committees and national party committees. By and large, congressional candidates in both parties and chambers have to rely on committees they create themselves for fund raising, research, and planning assistance.

Congressional elections occur under widely differing circumstances. In presidential years, turnout is relatively high and national issues can be invoked easily. In off years, however, only about half the eligible voters come out, and local issues often dominate the campaign. Thus the congressional elections occupy a unique place in the American political system. And this setting affects the way they are financed and regulated.

III. Development of Campaign Finance Regulation

Historically, American political parties and politics have been private, extralegal activities. When parties developed in the early 1800's they wrote their own rules, conducted their own primary elections, and set their own standards of behavior. In many places they conducted public elections, but almost no public laws regulated their activities until the second half of the nineteenth century.

When the public did intervene in the process of nominating candidates and conducting elections, its aim was usually to stop some particularly flagrant abuse, such as the Crédit Mobilier scandal of the nineteenth century when members of Congress received shares of stock for their favors. Legislative intervention has remained largely negative in character and intent. But the belief that politics is the public's business has been slowly growing for the last century, fostered by the courts, the press, the public, and sometimes even by the legislatures. Campaign finance regulation must be examined in this context.

Limits on Contributions by Public Employees

Contributions from public employees were a principal way to finance political activities during most of the nineteenth century. Each public employee was expected to give a certain percentage of his salary to his political party. Widespread abuses of the sale of public jobs led to a professional civil service and to protection of government employees from political solicitation. Candidates have been prohibited from soliciting campaign contributions from federal employees since 1867. The prohibition was strengthened in the Civil Service Reform Act of 1883 and again in the Hatch Act of 1939, which limits political activities of federal employees.[7]

In the states, practices still vary. The federal provision covers all government employees, federal, state, or local, whose salary comes in any part from the federal treasury.[8] Twenty states specifically prohibit solicitation of civil service employees. In others, state employees remain a regular and important source of funds for the political system.

Limits on Corporation and Union Contributions

As financing from government employees became more difficult, and large corporations became more seriously affected by governmental actions, politicians and corporations found cooperation increasingy beneficial. Mark Hanna, the Ohio industrialist who raised vast sums for William McKinley's campaigns, stated openly what many political fund raisers still hold as a goal: every corporation should "pay according to its stake in the general prosperity of the country and according to its special interest in the region...."[9]

By the end of the nineteenth century, businessmen and corporations had become important contributors to political campaigns. They needed help from government on tariffs, wage rates, taxes, banking policies, and in other areas. Politicians needed money as millions of immigrants and farmers arrived in the cities and had to be reached by the political system.

Demands for reform grew out of charges made during the presidential campaign of 1904. The Democratic candidate Alton B. Parker accused the Republicans of blackmailing corporations into contributing by threatening them with legal actions through the Bureau of Corporations. Though the Republicans received more than $2 million in direct contributions from corporations, President Theodore Roosevelt called Judge Parker's charge "a vicious falsehood."

After the election, the National Publicity Law Association, led by Perry Belmont, called for regulation of campaign finance. As one of the Democrats' principal fund raisers, Belmont was intimately aware of the corrupting relationships between corporate leaders and politicians. In his biography he reported that large contributors to political campaigns were among those most anxious for reform, presumably because buying the support of politicians was costing them too much.[10]

In 1907 President Roosevelt suggested a different approach to the problem of campaign finance—complete public subsidy. But the idea received only limited attention at the time. Instead Congress passed the Tillman Act of 1907 which prohibited corporations and national banks from making monetary political contributions. This legislation was consolidated into the first Corrupt Practices Act of 1910, modified in 1911 and still again in the Corrupt Practices Act of 1925.[11]

Soon another source of large political contributions emerged—organized labor. As the trade unions grew powerful in the 1930's their interests made them serious factors in federal political campaigns. Alexander Heard has placed labor contributions to politics in perspective:

> Much of the concern over organized labor in politics stems from its novelty. Business interests long dominated the politics of the nation—which is not to say the intent or the results were either bad or good—and more recently a new type of organized interest has entered the arena....
>
> It is more realistic to view the debate over labor's political finances as a struggle for the control of government than as a legal or moral issue. The debate may be waged in moral terms, and its result may be expressed in legal ones, but the origins and the stakes of the debate are the social and economic advantages that accompany political power.[12]

As labor unions grew in strength, number, resources, and political sophistication, demands arose that their political activities be curbed. The use of regular union treasury funds for political campaign contributions was first prohibited in the 1943 War Labor Disputes Act. The ban was extended to primary elections, conventions, and caucuses for federal nominations by the Taft-Hartley Act of 1947.[13] State laws have followed a pattern similar to that for federal laws. Thirty-four states have specific prohibitions on corporate contributions and four prohibit labor union contributions.[14]

A variety of techniques has been developed to evade the legal prohibitions against partisan political contributions by corporations and unions. Some corporations give high-level officers special bonuses which they are expected to contribute for use in political campaigns. Other corporations and some unions reimburse officers for political contributions and purchases of political dinner tickets through expense-account payments.[15] Corporations and unions contribute directly to campaigns for federal office through such subterfuges as purchasing postage stamps and giving them to campaign organizations. Corporations and unions frequently make illegal gifts in kind to campaigns, especially through the release of personnel and such facilities as sound trucks, telephone lines, computers, and office equipment.

Another frequent practice has been the paying of campaign bills, especially to public relations or advertising firms, as if they were expenses of the corporation or union. But recent Internal Revenue Service prosecutions of public relations firms that served as conduits for contributions, and of the organizations that paid them, may have made this route less appealing.[16]

A growing source of corporate money for campaigns during the 1960's was corporate advertising in essentially political publications. Under a favorable ruling by the Internal Revenue Service, corporations deducted the cost of the advertisements as a regular business expense. Corporate advertising in convention program books was a favorite way of helping finance national conventions. State parties also depend on corporate advertising. In Wisconsin, in 1964, the Democrats received 27.2 per cent ($191,441) of their funds this way while the Republicans tapped the same source (and probably the same companies) for 16.7 per cent ($179,750) of their funds.[17]

But the sale of advertising in political programs in 1964–65 by the Democratic National Committee caused objections among some advertisers and some opposition among politicians. Congress banned tax deductions for advertising in political journals in 1966. The ban was partially repealed in 1968 when the Congress realized that there was no adequate alternative immediately available to pay for the presidential nominating conventions. The 1966 ban was typical of the traditional approach to the regulation of finances. The 1968 repeal, however, represented a growing awareness in Congress that closing off sources of "undesirable" political money creates a need for adequate alternatives.

Limits on Individual Contributions

The federal Corrupt Practices Act sets a limit of $5,000 on contributions that may be made by an individual to a national political committee or to a candidate.[18] But these limitations have almost no practical effect on limiting individual contributions. What they do is diffuse responsibility for campaigns. The federal restriction has been interpreted to mean that no person can give more than $5,000 to any single committee. However, any number of committees can be formed to work for the election of a candidate. And an individual may make an unlimited number of $5,000 gifts to an unlimited number of political committees.

Similar provisions are contained in current state laws as chart 6 reveals. State limits are avoided in the same way as the federal statutes. Even in Florida, which has the most rigorous campaign finance regulations, a $1,000 limit on individual contributions is regularly avoided; Florida law does not require donors to certify that they are giving their own money, so single large contributions are often attributed to many people in $1,000 portions.

Limits on Total Spending

In addition to attempting to limit who may give and how much, federal and state laws have also tried to limit the amount of money spent by a political committee or candidate and the ways it can be spent. Neither limit has been effective, because neither has been realistic.

The federal limits—$5,000 for campaign committees for a Representative and $25,000 for a Senator—have little effect on campaign spending and no relation to the real needs of modern campaigns. Federal candidates establish many committees in support of their candidacy, each of which can spend up to the limit of $3 million. Or they use committees in their home state which are not affected by the federal statutes.

Twenty-seven states try to limit spending by enumerating legitimate campaign expenditures. Almost all proscribe one or more different types of expenditures. All states, for example, prohibit bribery and almost every state outlaws practices like vote buying.[19] (See chart 6.) Beyond these, however, the proscribed uses of money reflect the same *ad hoc* approach that marks so much of the legislation in this area, and tend to be as inconsistent. For example, while fourteen states prohibit spending to take voters to the polls, others specifically name that service as a legitimate campaign expenditure. (One of the reform proposals made by the Senate in 1967 in H.R. 4890 would add a federal ban on transporting voters to the polls.) Which policy better serves the public's interest in broad participation in the political system?

New Jersey had limits of $15,000 for House candidates and $100,000 for Senate candidates until the summer of 1969. The legislature repealed the limits when a defeated candidate in the gubernatorial primary, which also had a $100,000 limit, asked the court to declare the election void because the winning candidate freely admitted to spending more than $100,000.[20] No substantive reform was accomplished by removing the limit, but at least it took off the books a law that unrealistically limited spending and therefore was regularly flouted. ·

Nine states still base their spending limits on a percentage of the salary paid to a member of Congress. This type of limit fails the public interest in at least two ways: it is too low, and it encourages the masking of actual spending. Furthermore, limiting congressional campaign spending on the basis of salary fails to relate the money invested in a congressional election to its return to the political system, not merely to the candidate running for office.

Limits on who may give and how much may be spent in congressional campaigns have in fact failed to curb political spending. These limits have given expression to a general negative attitude toward politics. They have forced candidates to obscure the sources of their campaign contributions and thus have prevented the public from getting accurate information about who is paying the bills for political campaigns. Candidates have felt it necessary to set up multiple committees to finance their campaigns and publicly to deny responsibility for campaign financing.

Traditional Public Disclosure Regulations

Full public disclosure of campaign contributions and expenditures has often been viewed as the great antiseptic of politics. Its advocates believe it will keep campaigns free of the potential evils of big money.

It is true, of course, that if genuine full-disclosure statutes were enacted and enforced, the public would get some useful information to help judge its politicians' obligations and potential behavior. However, disclosure of information in a filed report is not in any sense equivalent to dissemination or to its use. To be effective, it must get to the voters before an election.

Discussion of the impact of full disclosure remains theoretical because the combination of current federal and state campaign finance reporting laws fails to reveal much, let alone disseminate it to the voters in a timely and useful manner. Current laws may be worse than none because they provide the appearance of both regulation and disclosure without much of the substance of either.

The federal government began requiring financial reports in the Corrupt Practices Act of 1910. Since that time national political committees, their subsidiaries, and federal candidates have been required to file reports on campaign income and expenditures. These political committees are required to report quarterly and then fifteen and five days before national elections.[21] These reports must include names, addresses, amounts, and dates of contributions of all donors of more than $100 in any year. The committees must also report the total amount of money they receive and itemize all expenditures over $10.

Candidates for federal office are required to report all contributions made directly to them for general election campaign purposes and all expenses made with their personal knowledge.[22] Expenses for primaries and other nominating procedures are specifically excluded from reporting requirements by the Corrupt Practices Act.[23] National committees and candidates for the House file their reports with the Clerk of the House of Representatives while Senate candidates file with the Secretary of the Senate. Individuals who spend more than $50 a year to influence elections in more than two states are also required to report their expenditures to the Clerk of the House.[24]

The federal reporting system is so inadequate that even after many years of reporting it is still impossible to develop anything more than a very rough estimate of how much money is spent on congressional campaigns. For example, total spending reported at the federal level for all 1968 congressional campaigns was $8,482,857. Actual spending, according to expert estimates, was in excess of $50 million.[25]

In 1968 total spending reported at the federal level for thirty-four Senate races was $2,714,464. In California alone, however, more than $4 million was reported to the Secretary of State by the candidates in the Senate primaries and general election.[26] Similarly, the amount reported ($5,768,393) for all the 435 House races is only a little more than twice the estimated amount spent on one House race alone. (The manager of one losing campaign admitted privately that $2 million was spent in the effort. There is almost no limit if men with money decide to "spend whatever it takes.")

Despite a widely acknowledged increase in campaign costs, the amount reported at the federal level for congressional campaigns in 1968 actually declined $689,032 from the $9,161,889 reported after the 1964 elections.[27] This is additional evidence that much if not most of the money spent on congressional elections goes unreported. Interstate committees file, but most campaigns are conducted through committees organized only in the candidate's own state. Candidates must report income and expenditures they know about, but many merely sign disclaimers saying they knew nothing about the financing of their elections.

As a result, many candidates file federal reports that list no expenditures. In 1968, 182 candidates for Congress filed reports stating they had no personal campaign income or expenditures and no committee expenditures that had to be reported at the federal level.[28] Some who reported nothing or little at the federal level filed state reports of over $500,000.[29] No reports of any kind were available from forty-one congressional candidates in 1968.

Those reports that are filed are not necessarily of much value. Federal reports are considered to be "verified" by the oaths of the people submitting them.[30] No audit or other independent verification of the information is required. Reports are open to the public for two years after they are filed, but researchers have reported that even during those two years they have had difficulty getting them. What is more, they are difficult to use because there are no prescribed reporting forms. Some candidates and committees submit long lists of names and addresses of donors accumulated by date. Others submit

ate copies of all their receipts and pay-out vouchers. The only
shed summary is made by *Congressional Quarterly,* a private
cation, usually late in the year after the elections.

The federal Corrupt Practices Act has failed because of its vast
number of loopholes and for its lack of effective enforcement procedures. Candidates and committees file their reports with politically
appointed officials of the Congress.[31] These officials have no authority
to do anything about the reports, even if they wanted to. The law
does not even require them to notify the Justice Department when
reports have not been filed. In 1968, when the Clerk of the House did
notify the Justice Department about the failure of several presidential
committees to submit reports before the deadline, the election was
over before any action could be taken. (The missing reports finally
came in, and nothing happened.)

The Constitution reserves to the House and the Senate the right
to judge the elections and qualifications of their own members. In
several instances, the Senate and House, after lengthy investigations,
have refused to seat people wl ᵻ had been elected, because of campaign spending abuses. But not lately. The last serious challenge
based on excessive and illegal campaign expenditures occurred in
1927, when the Reid Committee investigated the election to the Senate of Republican William S. Vare of Pennsylvania. The committee
reported that somewhere between $785,000 and $837,000 was spent
on Vare's election, with a substantial share going for "poll watchers"
on election day. Though his opponent in the primary was said to have
spent even more than Vare, no action was taken since the Corrupt
Practices Act excluded primaries from its coverage. Vare was finally
seated after the two-year probe ended, but he resigned shortly
afterward.[32]

The record of silence since the Vare investigation in the face of
Senate and House races that may have cost $2 million or more clearly
signifies a changed outlook in the Congress. Such high-priced campaigns may violate the letter, and even the spirit, of law and custom.
But they do not yet seriously violate the senses of the public or of
politicians as to what is required for modern campaigning.

Behavioral research and common sense suggest that enforcement
left solely in the hands of politicians and their appointees is not likely
to yield great benefits to the public. This is not to say that politicians

cannot be trusted. Politics, like other professions, has a strong set of informal mores and standards. Studies of the House and Senate repeatedly describe the existence of a complex set of informal rules and a professional *esprit* among congressional colleagues of different parties and sharply divergent ideology.[33]

One of the norms of the political profession is a high regard for the public interest. But another, equally strong, is tolerance of other politicians' political problems. Politicians, especially members of Congress, are loyal to institutional norms of behavior but, like all modern professional groups, they are guided more by standards of conduct practiced by their contemporaries than by those of the institutions they inhabit. While they feel free to set ethical standards for appointed officials, members of Congress seem to prefer that each elected member be judged on election day by his constituents. (The value of election day as a check on behavior must be viewed in the light of the fact that congressional elections are dominated by incumbents.)

When individual members of the Congress "go too far," as Thomas J. Dodd was felt to have done recently, other politicians move to discipline them. The standard against which Dodd was judged was not really the legal or formal rules of the Senate. Rather, he was "charged" with violating the norms established by his fellow politicians. Similarly, in those few cases in which Congress has denied a seat to a candidate because of excessive campaign spending, its members were guided by their own sense of what was "too much" rather than by any legal prescription.

In 1969 there were fourteen federal indictments for violations of the Corrupt Practices Act. All were initiated outside the Congress. Most of the indictments grew from Internal Revenue Service investigations of public relations firms who, it turned out, had served as conduits for corporate contributions to federal campaigns. The Commissioner of Internal Revenue, Randolph Thrower, warned publicly in October 1969 that illegal corporate contributions would be prosecuted.[34] And, in February 1970, two federally subsidized shipping lines were found guilty of making illegal contributions to federal candidates. They were fined $50,000 each.[35] Still, the public may not be provided with the information to judge the behavior of its politicians. Even after the indictments against the shipping lines were issued, the Attorney General would not release the names of the candidates—including members of Congress—who received the illegal contributions, since he is not required to do so in such cases.[36]

State Disclosure Requirements

Some candidates say they do not file federal reports because they file at the state level. They argue that filing both state and federal reports is an unnecessary inconvenience. But state public disclosure laws, under present circumstances, are not a satisfactory alternative.[37]

Most state reporting laws are at least as inadequate as the federal laws. The first state public campaign reporting law was passed by New York in 1890. California began regulating political committees in 1893. Today forty-three states require some form of report on campaign contributions and expenditures. (Chart 6 provides a summary of the widely different provisions.)

As with the federal law, the net effect of the state statutes appears, if anything, to be negative. For they generally fail to deter prohibited contributions and expenditures, and they do not inform the public of the fiscal behavior of their candidates. Public disclosure laws in the states do not meet the test of providing for wide dissemination of timely information. Only nineteen states require reports prior to an election. Fifteen of them provide no standard forms, so comparison is almost impossible. In the others, reports are submitted only after the election. Seven states have no reporting laws at all, and twelve require reports of only the personal expense of candidates, not of their committees. Thus in nineteen states there is no financial information from campaign committees supporting candidates for federal office.

Even the reports that are technically public property are difficult to use. Three states publish summaries of campaign spending reports; some make reports available for relatively brief periods of time; still others restrict the photocopying of them. Some state officials refuse to give investigators general access to the reports, producing material only in response to specific questions. In Indiana, Missouri, and Michigan, reports are filed only where the candidate lives, making access difficult and expensive.

State campaign reporting laws face some of the same barriers to effective enforcement that have impaired the federal Corrupt Practices Act. Reports are filed with an elected or appointed official, usually the Secretary of State. Such officials are reluctant to investigate or publicize the reports filed with them. Nineteen states require that failures to file reports be reported to prosecutors, but only sixteen states provide for any auditing or reviewing procedure. And in only three states can individuals or small groups initiate proceedings against candidates for abuse of the campaign reporting laws.

Attempts to strengthen state campaign reporting laws have been sporadic and have met with mixed success. In 1951 Florida adopted a strong public disclosure law, dubbed the "who gave it—who got it" law. It has been credited with improving the level of public knowledge and understanding of political campaign costs and practices.

Florida: The Limits of Public Disclosure

There is nothing like a scandal to help get campaign reforms passed; scandals give the public a compelling reason to demand an alternative set of standards for ethical behavior by politicians. And that is how Florida[38] got its election finance reform.

In the campaign for Senate in 1950, the two Democratic contenders reported that they had spent no more than $100,000 apiece, but the word got around that their actual outlays had been nearer half a million each. The St. Petersburg *Times* got onto the story and turned it into a crusade for reform. On the heels of that came the Kefauver Committee's revelations about the gubernatorial campaign of 1948. One candidate, it turned out, received contributions of $150,000 from each of three men. And one of those contributors was a racetrack owner with connections to the Al Capone mob.

The Florida "who gave it—who got it" campaign finance law differs from most other state reporting laws in several ways. It places no limits on total spending for a campaign, but imposes a ceiling of $1,000 on individual contributions to any campaign for office in Florida. However, since individuals do not have to vouch that they are giving their own money, some have acted merely as conduits for other people's money.

Certain contributions are considered automatically to be suspect and are prohibited. For example, no gifts may be made by people with "vested economic interests" in dog- and horse-racing permits (three horse-track operators were charged with secret contributions

CHART 6

REGULATION OF CAMPAIGN CONTRIBUTIONS

State	Corporate contribs. prohibited	Labor union contribs. prohibited	Individual contribs. limited to	Solicitation from state employees prohibited (1)	Solicitation from candidates illegal	Contribs. under fictitious names illegal
Alabama	Yes			Yes	Yes	
Alaska						
Arizona	Yes					
Arkansas				(2)		
California				Yes		
Colorado						
Connecticut	Yes				Yes	Yes
Delaware						
Florida	Yes(3)		$1,000(3)		Yes	
Georgia	Yes					
Hawaii	Yes					
Idaho						
Illinois				(4)		
Indiana	Yes	Yes		Yes	Yes	Yes
Iowa	Yes			Yes		
Kansas	Yes(5)					
Kentucky	Yes			Yes		
Louisiana	Yes			Yes		
Maine						Yes
Maryland			$2,500			Yes
Massachusetts	Yes		(6)	Yes	Yes	Yes
Michigan	Yes				Yes	Yes
Minnesota	Yes				Yes	
Mississippi					Yes	
Missouri	Yes				Yes	
Montana	Yes		Yes(7)	Yes	Yes	Yes

1. Generally refers to employees under civil service or merit system.

2. It is unlawful for any person whomsoever to assess any state employee for any political purpose whatsoever, or to coerce by threats or otherwise any such employee into making a subscription or contribution for any such purpose.

3. The following persons also are prohibited from making campaign contributions, directly or indirectly:
    a. Holders of horse or dog racing permits;
    b. Holders of licenses for the sale of intoxicating beverages;
    c. Operators of public utilities, except nonprofit cooperatives.

4. State employees whose tenure is subject to merit principles are forbidden to engage in certain specified prohibited political activities *during working hours,* and the prohibited activities include soliciting money for political purposes and making contributions of money in behalf of candidates or in support of public or political issues. The prohibition does not apply to soliciting and making contributions *after working hours.*

5. Contributions by such corporations as banks, trusts, railroads, and utilities are forbidden.

6. Individual contributions during year are limited to $3,000 to one candidate, $3,000 to one party, and $3,000 to nonelected political committees not organized on behalf of any candidate.

7. Any person expending more than $50 in a campaign must file an itemized statement and give

State	Corporate contribs. prohibited	Labor union contribs. prohibited	Individual contribs. limited to	Solicitation from state employees prohibited(1)	Solicitation from candidates illegal	Contribs. under fictitious names illegal
Nebraska	Yes		$1,000(8)			
Nevada						
N. Hampshire	Yes	Yes	$5,000	(9)	Yes	
New Jersey	Yes			Yes	Yes	Yes
New Mexico						
New York	Yes			Yes	Yes	
No. Carolina	Yes					
No. Dakota	Yes				Yes	Yes
Ohio	Yes			Yes(10)	Yes	
Oklahoma	Yes					
Oregon	Yes(11)			Yes	Yes	Yes
Pennsylvania	Yes	Yes		(12)		Yes
Rhode Island						
So. Carolina						
So. Dakota	Yes					
Tennessee	Yes					
Texas	Yes	Yes		Yes		
Utah	Yes				Yes	
Vermont						
Virginia						
Washington						
West Virginia	Yes		$5,000	Yes	Yes	
Wisconsin	Yes			Yes	Yes	
Wyoming	Yes			Yes		
United States	Yes	Yes	$5,000(13)	Yes(14)		

a duplicate to the candidate or treasurer of the political organization whose success or defeat he has sought to promote.

8. No treasurer of a political committee shall receive or accept more than $1,000 from any one person to be spent in any one campaign.

9. Employees under civil service are not allowed to contribute money for the promotion of candidates or political issues.

10. Solicitation from civil servants prohibited and receipt of contributions from mine inspectors prohibited.

11. Contributions prohibited from banks, utility corporations, or a majority of their stockholders.

12. Contributions may not be solicited from civil service employees and those employed by the Game Commission and the Board of Parole.

13. $5,000 limitation applies only to contributions to a national committee during any calendar year, or in connection with any campaign for an elective federal office. Hatch Act specifically excludes contributions to state or local committees from this limitation.

14. Applies to federal employees or to persons receiving salary or compensation for services from money derived from the U.S. Treasury.

SOURCE: *Regulation of Political Finance,* Laura Penny and Herbert Alexander, Institute of Government, Berkeley, 1966.

this year), liquor licenses or profit-making public utility franchises. Corporate and union contributions are banned.

The Florida law also has a new kind of restriction to prevent a last-minute flood of unreported money. No contributions may be made in the five days before or after an election. And no campaign may go into debt in the expectation that money will be raised after the election.

The Florida law assigns responsibility for all campaign actions to the candidate and his appointed representatives. Before a candidate is placed on the ballot, he must designate a campaign treasurer authorized to receive and spend campaign funds and a central depository bank into which all campaign contributions are to be deposited within twenty-four hours after receipt. (For statewide campaigns, a sub-agent and bank may be designated for each county.)

No expenditures may be made on behalf of any candidate for office unless they are authorized by him or his treasurer. This provision has been subjected to criticism as possible violation of the constitutional protection of free speech. However, the Florida Supreme Court held in 1953 that requiring campaign expenditures to be cleared through the candidate's treasurer and strictly accounted for was a legitimate exercise of the police power of the state.

Candidates are required to file reports of contributions and expenditures on forms supplied by the state. Candidates for the United States Senate must file reports weekly while candidates for House seats and political committees must file monthly. Campaign organizations for all offices must file final reports fifteen days after each primary or general election. And all reports must be filed both in the home county of candidates and with the Secretary of State. Penalties for failing to file are severe, ranging from a misdemeanor to loss of office. But the Secretary of State is not obliged to initiate action or inform the Attorney General that candidates have failed to file or have filed improperly. The entire question of enforcement was left in doubt when the law was passed in 1951. Four years later, the law was modified to allow individual citizens to initiate action if they believed its provisions had been violated. Upon receipt of an individual's complaint, the Attorney General must determine what, if any, action should be taken. This right of individual action has been used successfully several times.

The Florida law does not require the state to publicize the reports or distribute summaries of them. But the state's political press corps has assumed the job of providing quick exposure of the reported material. The law clearly gives the public more information about its political candidates' behavior than it got before. Further, the law clearly establishes the responsibility of candidates for what their supporters claim. Disclaimers of responsibility for charges or promises made by overzealous but uncontrolled supporters in the heat of a campaign can no longer be made in Florida. Candidates and potential contributors alike are protected from unauthorized promises made to contributors by fund raisers, such as those allegedly made by Bobby Baker to the California Savings and Loan Association, whose members, according to testimony at the Baker trial, contributed $66,000 for campaigns at Baker's request, none of which was turned over to the campaigns.[39]

Florida's campaign reporting law has probably strengthened the political process as a whole by informing the electorate of the real costs of the political system. Florida's citizens are probably more aware now of the role of campaign spending in the political system. This awareness, in fact, led to an experimental law to shorten campaigns to eight weeks as a way of bringing costs down. It was tried in 1958 but did not work; candidates just spent money faster. The law was repealed.

While the campaign reporting law has been judged a success, Florida's experience indicates that even genuine full disclosure is not a complete solution to all the problems of campaign finance. First, the greater publicity has not changed the distribution of political resources; it has merely exposed it. Candidates who had inadequate resources before still do. Second, the law has not made any noticeable contribution to recruiting and presenting genuine alternative leaders and policies. In fact, some observers believe the disclosure law has reduced the number of candidates running for office because everyone now knows how much money it really takes to run a campaign.

A few other states have followed the example of the Florida law —with varying results. Massachusetts adopted a Florida-type statute in 1962. Observers feel that it has not had a great impact. Critics claim that the reports filed by Massachusetts candidates still do not reflect actual campaign expenditures. They also state that the pre-election reports have received little attention from the press of the state.[40]

Federalism and Congressional Campaign Regulation

Article I, Section 4, Paragraph 1, of the Constitution provides:

The times, places, and manner of holding elections for Senators and Representatives shall be prescribed in each state by the legislature thereof; but the Congress may at any time by law make or alter such regulations, except as to the places of choosing Senators.

As a result, congressional campaign finance has fallen between federal and state legislation. For example, the activities of political committees in nineteen states receive no public scrutiny at all. In other states political campaigns have been conducted in ways that avoid both state and federal reporting requirements. In federal campaigns, political committees are frequently established in one state that does not require reports to transfer funds into another state that does. Contributions from outside a state may be reported as transfers, with either no indication of the source or an uninformative political committee name. In 1968, Representative George H. Fallon (Dem., Md.), Chairman of the Public Works Committee, received over $40,000 in campaign contributions from outside his state. This represented two-thirds of his campaign budget. The real sources for major portions of these contributions were never reported.[41] Representative Edward A. Garmatz (Dem., Md.), Chairman of the Merchant Marine and Fisheries Committee, included in his 1968 state reports of campaign receipts over $38,000 from the kind of high-priced receptions that Washington lobbyists attend, or at least pay for. The state report did not name any of the groups that bought blocks of tickets to the receptions. But searches of separate reports, filed by political committees in Washington, traced about $4,000 to labor union committees active in industries regulated by the Congressman's committee; other blocks of tickets were bought by representatives of businesses in the same heavily subsidized industry.[42]

The money raised through these means was not by itself necessarily "evil" or tainted. Most of the money contributed to the campaigns cited here probably went to pay for services that are essential to the successful operation of a democratic political system. Some of the money was used for voter registration and voter education. Some was undoubtedly used to help insure the smooth and orderly operation of the voting places on election day. Other manpower and money resources were probably devoted to get-out-the-vote drives which brought voters to the polls who might not have participated otherwise.

Federal and state sharing of responsibility for supervising campaign finance has led to other abuses. Corporations, prohibited from contributing to federal campaigns, can still contribute to state and local campaigns in sixteen states. In many of these states it is common practice for corporate contributions to federal campaigns to be funneled through local party committees. Union contributions follow the same route in even more states.

In short, the political system operates on a national scale. National contributions to local congressional campaigns have grown remarkably fast in recent years. They are now a major source of congressional campaign funds, and this trend is likely to continue. The economic and political issues that motivate this growth of contributions do not respect local and state boundaries.

The federal government may need to exercise its constitutional option of federal supremacy to regulate the conduct of congressional campaigns. Only with adequate national reporting will the public be able to get full information about the functional roles of congressional representatives. Similarly, a level of responsibility for campaign behavior high enough to offset public doubts about congressional campaign spending may be possible only through a set of national standards. In recent years some effort has been made to increase federal responsibility.

Recent Developments at the Federal Level

Attempts have been made to refine and strengthen the traditional weapons of regulation: contribution and expenditure limits and public disclosure. At the same time, other attempts have been made either to broaden or to change entirely the base of political campaign contributions. One such approach suggests redistributing to other parts of the society some of the political system's costs that are now carried privately by campaigns. These approaches do not necessarily contradict each other. But the different approaches raise basic questions about the nature and direction of our political system, and elements of all three approaches will probably be needed to answer them.

Improving Federal Reporting

The current federal Corrupt Practices Act has been shown to be weak and ineffective. Advocates of full public disclosure still insist, with a good deal of pontification, that their approach has not yet been given a full test. Since 1948 several attempts have been made to revise spending limits and strengthen reporting requirements of the federal laws. At the same time, however, court decisions have worked to undermine the effect of many of the restrictions, and donors have been considerably more successful at finding ways around the laws than reformers have been at tightening them.

Although the general public remains in favor of ceilings on campaign expenditures,* politicians have pressed to eliminate or raise them. Several congressional reports have cited current limits as open invitations to criminal violations. Various recommendations for change have been proposed from time to time but none have yet been adopted.

In its report on the 1948 elections, the House Committee on Campaign Expenditures recommended that limits on campaign expenditures be raised substantially.[43] In 1951 a special House committee that investigated the 1950 elections urged that the limits be repealed. It also recommended that primary elections be included within the scope of federal law and that political committees be prohibited from receiving and spending funds without authorization from the candidate they claimed to support. The 1951 report called for a repeal or liberalization of the prohibitions of the Hatch Act against participation of federal employees in election campaigns.

In 1953, 1955, and 1957, the Senate Committee on Rules and Administration and its subcommittee on congressional elections proposed formulas for raising the limits for congressional campaign and political committee spending.

In 1960 a bill (S. 2436) which combined higher limits and stricter standards for public disclosure passed the Senate but was not acted on in the House.[44] A similar but more modest bill (S. 2426) was passed again by the Senate in 1961 but died in the House.[45]

President Kennedy's Commission on Campaign Costs recommended that upper limits both on spending and on individual cam-

---

*According to the Gallup poll, 71 per cent favored limits in 1965, 1966, and 1967, and 67 per cent favored limits in May 1968.

58

paign contributions be dropped.[46] The commission also recommended tighter reporting regulations, at least for presidential campaigns, and the establishment of a Registry of Election Finance to help enforce financial regulations and improve dissemination of information. Bills submitted to Congress by the President in 1962 and 1963 called for enactment of all the recommendations of the commission. None were approved until 1964 when a special transition fund was established which later smoothed the arrival of the Nixon administration and the departure of the Johnson administration.[47] The transition fund act represents a step toward removing some of the noncampaign costs of the political system away from private campaign funds.

President Johnson called for a stronger federal public disclosure statute in his State of the Union Message of 1966.[48] He urged that spending limits on political committees and candidates be eliminated so that the proliferation of committees in support of a candidate would be discouraged. He asked that primary elections and state and local political committees be included in the federal reporting requirements and that firm penalties for violating the laws be enacted.

In his May 1966 message on federal campaign finance, President Johnson joined the problems of congressional ethics and political campaign funds by asking, in vain, that members of Congress be required to disclose all payments of $100 or more received for personal services to nongovernment agencies.[49] Campaign contributions from businesses, trade associations, and unions have often been disguised in the form of honoraria for speeches, particularly for incumbents.

A bill passed in the Senate in 1967 (S. 1880) made several changes in the Corrupt Practices Act.[50] Elections were redefined to include primaries, caucuses, and conventions. The requirement to file was broadened to include every political committee intrastate or interstate that spent over $1,000 in any year. Any political committee expecting to spend more than $1,000 in a year would have to register upon its formation. A political contribution was redefined to include loans and gifts of anything of value.

The kind and detail of information to be reported were also expanded. Transfers of funds among political committees and loans to committees would be more carefully reported. The bill mandated forms for the reports and a manual of recommended uniform accounting procedures. Reports were to be filed, as before, with the Secretary of the Senate and the Clerk of the House, with copies filed with the clerk of the district court where the committee or candidate had headquarters.

The Senate bill recognized the distinction between disclosure of information and its dissemination. Therefore the Secretary of the Senate and the Clerk of the House were directed to prepare and publish annual summaries of the reports; to publish special analyses of the information from time to time; to keep a current list of all statements that pertained to any candidate; to make the reports available for public inspection and copying; and to "assure wide dissemination of statistics, summaries and reports prepared under the act."

A potential major weakness of the bill was the retention of enforcement initiative in the hands of officers of the Congress, dependent on its members' approval for their jobs. Senator Hugh Scott and Senator Joseph Clark urged that investigatory and enforcement powers be vested either in a bipartisan independent federal elections commission or in the General Accounting Office.[51]

The 1967 Senate bill proposed to continue the tradition of deferring to the states with respect to campaign regulation. Thus, for example, while the bill would have repealed federal ceilings on spending, it would have allowed individual states to maintain their own unrealistically low ceilings.

The House Administration Committee also considered its own extensive disclosure reform bill in 1967–68 (finally numbered H.R. 11233 and referred to as the Ashmore-Goodell bill).[32] The bill was stalled in committee by an unusual coalition of Southern conservative Democrats and urban liberal Democrats. The Southerners objected to the bill's inclusion of primaries while the urban representatives feared that a provision against use of union and corporate funds to pay the operating expenses of political action committees would reduce labor contributions to their campaigns. The bill remained pigeonholed in the Rules Committee, even after removal of the provision objected to by urban Democrats.

The major features of the bill passed by the Senate in 1967, the House bill, and the current provisions of the Corrupt Practices Act are compared in the Appendix. The House bill provided for a five-man bipartisan federal elections commission to receive, audit, and

60

publicize the reports, and to hold hearings on disputed reports. After a finding of fact, it could order the committee affected to file a corrected report. It also provided more stringent requirements for information to be included in the reports. Purchasers of tickets totalling $100 or more for fund-raising events were to be reported by full name and mailing address under the House bill but not under the Senate version.

The House bill reflected controversies over ethics which have rocked the Congress in recent years. A specific prohibition against personal use of campaign contributions from fund-raising events by candidates or members of Congress was included. Each member of Congress was to be required to make an annual statement listing the sources of any gifts and honoraria exceeding $100 to him or his family. Candidates for Congress were also to file such reports ten to fifteen days before the election.

While the House bill eliminated spending limits for campaigns and political committees, it attempted to tighten limitations on individual contributions. No individual could give more than $5,000 in the aggregate to any single campaign.

No final action was taken by the Congress on either the Senate bill or the Ashmore-Goodell House bill during the 90th Congress. Ramsey Clark, then Attorney General, submitted proposed legislation similar to the House bill to the Congress shortly before he left office.[53] No hearings on any changes were held in either house of Congress during 1969.

This brief review of recent developments points out some of the problems and prospects for campaign finance-reporting reform. A consensus seems slowly to be emerging among the professional politicians that the public must get more information about campaign financing. However, Congressmen are understandably reluctant to upset current methods of avoiding limitations on the use of corporate and union funds in campaigns unless they are assured that adequate money will be available to meet campaign needs from other sources. Public disclosure implies something may be wrong with the current system of political finance, but offers no alternative structure.

IV. Changing the Base of Political Finance

The trend in twentieth-century federal campaign finance toward greater reliance on relatively small numbers of large contributors, that is on rich individuals and well-endowed special interest groups, creates a major weakness in the political system.

Public opinion polls have consistently shown that about 30 to 40 per cent of the American people say they would be willing to make a small political contribution if asked.[54] The success of mass contribution drives on behalf of the United Fund and other charities impelled politicians, businessmen, union leaders, and foundations in the early 1950's to attempt to broaden the base of political contributors in the same way. But in almost twenty years these efforts have produced little. About 35 per cent of the voters interviewed in 1968 said they would be willing to make a contribution, but only 8 per cent reported that they actually did. This is one-third more than the proportion who said they actually contributed in 1954.[55]

Since 1952, the growth of individual small contributors to politics, especially to the Republican party and to the George Wallace movement, has differed only slightly from the growth of the population and the rise in campaign expenditures. While the relative importance of the small giver has increased in the Republican party, it has declined dramatically in the Democratic party. The Democrats now rely much more heavily on large contributors than they did in the 1950's. Chart 7 indicates these trends on a national level.[56]

CHART 7

**CONTRIBUTIONS OF $500 OR MORE AS PER CENT OF ALL CONTRIBUTIONS
BY INDIVIDUALS TO NATIONAL-LEVEL COMMITTEES, DEMOCRATIC
AND REPUBLICAN PARTIES, 1952-1968**

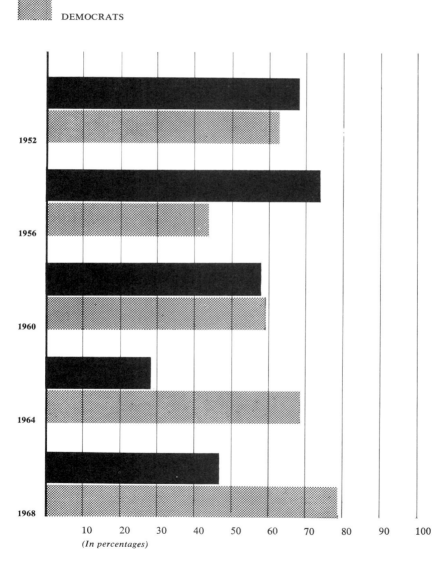

REPUBLICANS

DEMOCRATS

SOURCE: *Voters' Time.* Twentieth Century Fund Commission on Campaign Costs in the
Electronic Era, The Twentieth Century Fund, New York, 1969.
NOTE: 1969 estimated on basis of preliminary data.

Mass Bipartisan Appeals

Much of the effort to broaden the base of contributions has concentrated on the idea that political giving is socially desirable. One approach has been by bipartisan efforts. Prior to the 1958, '60, '62 and '64 elections, the American Heritage Foundation and the Advertising Council conducted a nationwide advertising campaign encouraging people to "give a buck" to the party or candidate of their choice. Both the Democratic and Republican parties conducted door-to-door fund-raising drives across the country.

But a private poll taken after the 1958 election showed no increase from 1954 to 1958 in the percentage (6 per cent) of the people who said they actually made a political contribution. The Survey Research Center studies of the presidential election years 1960 and 1964 did show increases—10 per cent and 12 per cent respectively reported giving.

In 1964 a nationwide bipartisan mail appeal was initiated at the suggestion of R. L. Polk and Company, a direct-mail advertising concern. Former President Dwight D. Eisenhower and Ambassador Adlai Stevenson served as co-chairmen of the drive. An impressive group of notables from the Democratic and Republican parties made up the organizing committee.[57] But test mailings to 300,000 households proved disappointing, and the proposed nationwide effort was abandoned.

The designers of the experiment concluded that its bipartisan approach may have been one of the reasons for the failure. That conclusion seems to have been supported by the fact that while the Eisenhower-Stevenson experiment was failing, the partisan Goldwater campaign was raising large sums from small mailed contributions. In 1964 the Republicans raised 32 per cent of their national committee money from direct mail.

No bipartisan nationwide fund-raising drive has taken place since the 1964 experiment. Partisan direct-mail campaigns have, however, become important sources of political funds, especially for the Republicans. Since 1964 the Republican National Committee has continued to cultivate mail contributions, and these play an important role in meeting operating expenses. Such contributions helped the Republican party gain an early and impressive lead in fund raising over the Democrats in the 1968 presidential campaign.

Democratic direct-mail fund raising has been significantly less successful. Between 1960 and 1968 the Democratic National Committee paid little attention to the method. Its program barely covered its costs. In 1969 it tried a direct-mail program which was unsuccessful. A new effort was launched early in 1970. Meanwhile Democratic congressional campaign committees have had modest success with direct-mail drives for the 1970 elections.

Door-to-Door Fund Raising

Door-to-door solicitation by neighbors on the model of the United Fund has also been tried both by bipartisan and partisan groups. The few reported results of bipartisan door-to-door drives have not indicated marked success. A community-wide experiment in Saginaw, Michigan, in 1964 was a particularly dismal failure.[58] Despite broad civic and political support, detailed planning, and extensive publicity, a one night door-to-door canvass raised only $410.86 from 372 of the 6,830 voters covered, nowhere near the $2,800 administrative grant, the staff time, and the value of the advertising media invested in the drive.

Partisan door-to-door fund raising has a spotty but somewhat better record. Both parties have reported stunning failures and successes. Each has a few counties it can use to show that the technique can work. In Hennepin County (Minneapolis), for example, the Republican neighbor-to-neighbor drive raised $40,971 in 1958; annual drives now raise over $250,000 for the party.[59] The Democrats can turn to Montgomery County, Maryland, as one example of successful door-to-door solicitation. In 1960 volunteer solicitors raised $32,000 in the county and in 1968 they brought in $36,000.[60]

A spokesman for the George Wallace campaign offered no breakdowns of finances by sources, size of contribution, or in any other way. He asserted, however, that the bulk of Wallace campaign funds in 1968 came in the form of small gifts through the mail, usually following appearances by the candidate, and a relatively small amount came as a result of specific direct-mail solicitation.

Corporate Nonpartisan Programs

Corporate political fund-raising programs have scored outstanding successes and failures. But company-wide nonpartisan efforts have not been as fruitful as other methods, such as funds established by higher salaried executives.[61] Company-wide programs seem to fail because they offer little incentive for most employees. Gifts are passed on to candidates and parties in the name of the company rather than the giver, who gets no recognition for his contribution. Corporate public affairs officers complain that not enough money is raised to justify the effort. In fact, the programs often cost as much as they raise. Other corporations have developed successful programs. Hughes Aircraft, for example, got about 25 per cent of its employees to contribute an average of $12 during the 1968 drive,[62] on which the company had invested considerable promotional effort.

Corporate officials believe their companies derive important benefits from these nonpartisan campaign contribution programs. The programs generate favorable free publicity for the company. Companies also gain political benefits because management representatives get to know many candidates, and candidates become acquainted with the company.

Political funds from high salaried corporate employees have raised substantial amounts of money for congressional campaigns in recent years. Procedures vary from company to company, but management or good government funds have been established in almost every major American corporation.[63] In most, salaried executives who make more than $15,000 a year are invited—often unofficially compelled—to join by contributing a small percentage, perhaps 0.5 per cent or 1 per cent of their annual salary. These funds raise substantial amounts of money early in a campaign year when money is most needed. Many of these corporate programs are carried on with little fanfare. Most are informal and few are registered as formal political committees.

While these corporate programs are ostensibly nonpartisan, they raise more money for Republicans than for Democrats, just as labor's nonpartisan COPE (Committee On Political Education) drives raise more money for Democrats than Republicans.

COPE Drives

Labor union contributions to political campaigns are usually viewed as large donations even though they generally result from large numbers of small contributions by union members. The aggregating process used by COPE recognizes a political reality: large contributions, and their contributors, are sought and noticed. Small contributions are not.

Operating expenses and the costs of political education and voter registration programs come from regular union funds. But contributions to partisan campaigns and candidates must come from voluntary contributions of union members.

Each year in local COPE drives union members are asked to donate $1.00 or more to their union's political action commmittee. Contributions are made in cash, and the donors get COPE receipts. COPE estimates that no more than 25 per cent of all union members are asked in any year.[64] Some of the money is sent to COPE for national campaigns and some is used in local contests. The program works with varying effectiveness. The Communications Workers regularly have more than 100 per cent participation (some members give more than $1.00). The UAW Citizenship Fund has high participation in part because members contribute through payroll deductions. Some unions have no drives at all.

COPE drives differ from corporate company-wide programs in a major way. Corporate nonpartisan drives often emphasize good government and citizenship. COPE drives are usually hard-hitting calls to the fight for working men's social and economic needs. COPE donates almost all of its money to liberal Democrats.

Corporate and Union Programs and the Public Interest

Corporations and unions appear to be better able than the political parties to raise large numbers of small contributions. They have regular and effective contact with employees and members, and they have a framework for stimulating donations. In contrast, most political committees do not.

Corporate and union political education and solicitation programs have become substitutes for political party activity, but it remains to be seen if they can serve the variety of interests a successful political party serves. The work place represents only one of the interests people have, and it may operate to the detriment of their other interests.

A great deal more ought to be known about the impact of institutional settings on the nature and direction of political involvement before voluntary corporate and union drives are permitted to become the principal means for raising money for politics. Would the money flow to different candidates and policies if the same people were giving in a different institutional framework, such as a church or a parent-teacher association? Many observers believe it would.

The public interest may not be well served if political fund raising is assigned to narrowly focused, essentially nonpolitical institutions, even though more people participate.

Tax Incentives

Tax incentives to encourage political contributions have been suggested with increasing frequency as a way to broaden the base of political finance. Tax incentives, supporters argue, would make giving to politics as respectable as giving to churches and charities.

President Kennedy's Commission on Campaign Costs recommended in 1962 that political contributors get either a tax credit of 50 per cent of contributions up to a total credit of $10 or a tax deduction for contributions up to $1,000 made to a national or state party committee.[65]

Since then, several variations have been offered. The basic plan involves either a tax credit or a tax deduction, or a combination of the two. The maximum credit or deduction varies, and the authorized recipients change. In these proposals, contributions can be restricted to political parties, as the President's commission suggested, or to candidate committees, or to both.

Those who argue for tax incentives feel that they would be a cue to the mass of the population that political contributions are recommended by the government. Objections have been based on practical considerations, real or imaginary. Some believe deductions and credits will be claimed by people who did not actually make any political contributions. Others fear that tax incentives would be used as a new form of political scrip to pay off the party faithful, buy votes, and otherwise make the political system less honest than it is now.

To overcome such objections, a number of gimmicks have been devised: special receipts, vouchers, special political money orders, or special stamps have been recommended. To preserve an individual's anonymity some have suggested creating an independent agency as an intermediary between donor and candidate or committee.

Each elaboration of the tax incentive program designed to overcome problems seems to create new and more complex ones. States that now have tax deduction provisions have attempted to keep them relatively simple. California and Minnesota treat political deductions like any other; the taxpayer must be prepared to justify his deductions. Missouri requires that receipts from a political committee be submitted by the taxpayer claiming the deduction.

Tax Deductions and Credits

The choice of what tax incentive to offer, credit or deduction, has an important bearing on the kind of contributors who will benefit from the incentive. Tax deductions benefit those in higher income brackets more than those in lower income brackets. Under the progressive income tax, a contribution of $100 by a man in the 50 per cent marginal bracket "costs" him less than the same $100 given by a man in the 15 per cent bracket. Furthermore, tax deductions are available only to those who itemize deductions on their tax forms. This would eliminate half of the federal income taxpayers who do not itemize deductions. (President Johnson's 1966 proposal tried to overcome this inequity by making the deduction for political contributions available with the standard deduction.)

Five states now allow limited tax deductions for political contributions.[66] In California, in 1969, 4.3 million tax returns were filed, and 47 per cent used the standard deduction, eliminating the opportunity for a political deduction. (As with federal figures, users of the standard deduction correlated closely with those of lower incomes.)[67] Somewhere between 100,000 and 150,000 of the remainder entered a deduction for a political contribution of up to the maximum of $100. There was a much greater frequency of entering a political deduction at higher income levels. Those with lower incomes took considerably less than the maximum allowed.[68]

Because limited information is available, it is impossible to generate even a rough guess of how much money was actually contributed and deducted from state income tax returns. And it is impossible to determine how much money was given because of the tax incentive and how much would have been contributed in any case.

Tax credits benefit lower income rather than higher income people: a $10 or $20 credit is obviously a greater percentage of a $200 tax bill in taxes than it is of a $2,000 tax bill. To retain the element of personal involvement, proponents often urge that a credit be given only for a percentage of contributions, up to a maximum. For example, the tax credit might be for 50 per cent of contributions up to $20 for an individual return. The donor would give $20 to a political committee and claim a $10 credit on his tax return. In this way he would be giving $10 of his "own" money and $10 that would have gone to the government.

Only Oregon currently allows a tax credit for political contributions. As of January 1, 1970, taxpayers may claim a tax credit for 50 per cent of contributions up to $10 for a single return and to $20 for a joint return. Creditable contributions may be made to committees for any candidate on an official ballot in a primary or general election or to any political party.

Tax Incentives and the Public Interest

It is not yet clear whether tax incentives would attract new money into the system. Some political practitioners argue that local leadership, partisanship, sound organization, hard work by volunteers, and continuity are the determinants of success in soliciting massive numbers of small political contributions. They also do not believe that a person will be persuaded to give a small contribution by a solicitor's explanation of a tax device that would allow him to recover all or part of his donation. The principal weakness of tax incentives, they argue, is that they do not address the real problem. Since 35 to 40 per cent of the population has already indicated it will give, without a tax incentive, the solution ought to offer a way to collect the money. Most tax incentive proposals have nothing to do with the problem of creating a mechanism that could collect money from millions of people.

The use of any or all of these techniques to broaden citizen participation in political finance may help solve some of the problems of the rising costs of campaigns. But they have not yet replaced large donors. Political campaigners need all the money they can get, whether it is raised in small or large sums. Even though there were several hundred thousand small givers to the Republican party in 1968, more than $18 million came from fewer than 10,000 donors, in amounts of $500 or more. Those who would seek to replace the presence and influence of large donors in political campaigns have not yet found a solution. So large donations continue to dominate political finance.

Public Subsidies for Federal Political Campaigns

Recognition that large donations continue to dominate political finance has led a number of political practitioners and theorists to support some form of direct or indirect public subsidy as the only practical alternative. Proponents of public subsidy believe that no amount of regulation or public disclosure can produce a strong political system that fairly presents the voters with alternative candidates and policies.

The case for subsidizing political campaigns does not rest only on opposition to private finance or functional representation. Rather, its supporters argue that public subsidies should be provided because not enough money is now being spent to maintain a strong democratic political system.[69] Even some strong supporters of functional representation, like Senator Russell B. Long, have called for public subsidies for political campaigns.[70] Senator Long best described why supporters of public subsidies find the current pattern of political finance unacceptable, even with the prospect of many small contributors:

> I am frank to tell you that I sometimes gain the impression that when you are talking in terms of large campaign contributions—I do not mean the $100 type, I mean the big ones, $5,000 and above—the distinction between a campaign contribution and a bribe is almost a hair's line difference. You can hardly tell one from the other.
>
> For example, I recall an election in my state where one man put up almost a quarter of a million dollars. He was a very fine, high type man and we passed a big tax that cost him a fortune. But we did not do that without first talking to him and saying, we think this is necessary, we hope you will pardon us for doing it. Frankly, if he had said, no, no, it just cannot be done, I do not know whether we would have done that or not....[71]

Direct Public Financial Subsidies

In 1907 President Theodore Roosevelt, responding to the controversy over the influence of corporate contributions, recommended that political campaigns be paid for by public rather than by private funds. His proposal was rejected in favor of the limitation and disclosure approach. The special Senate committee that investigated campaign expenditures in the 1936 elections also recommended that private contributions to federal campaigns be barred completely and that campaigns be financed by the government, but no action was taken.

In 1966 the Presidential Election Campaign Fund was enacted (Title III of Public Law 89-809). This law allowed each taxpayer, by checking a box on his return, to have one dollar of his taxes paid into a special fund to pay for presidential elections. The funds were to be used to reimburse major and minor parties for legitimate campaign expenses. The act gave equal funds to major parties (defined as those gaining more than fifteen million votes in the previous presidential election), and minor parties (between five and fifteen million votes in the previous election) were to receive shares based on the number of votes they had gained.[72] The Comptroller General and an advisory board were to determine the legitimacy of expenses and would order the Treasury to make payments.

While there was limited public debate on the measure when it was passed in 1966, the fight to repeal or suspend it in 1967 consumed five weeks of debate on the Senate floor.[73] The repeal fight was led by Senator Albert Gore of Tennessee, who favored a much more comprehensive reform of campaign finance and regulation than the bill accomplished, and by Senator John J. Williams of Delaware.

The Senate was closely divided. Neither side would admit defeat,[74] and several test votes were taken. The impasse was broken finally when Senator Mike Mansfield moved to have the Presidential Campaign Fund Act suspended until guidelines on its use were enacted into law. Senator Long predicted the fund would be in operation for the 1968 elections, and Senator Williams pronounced the fund dead.[75] Senator Williams proved the more accurate prophet, at least to date.

Those who favored the 1966 Presidential Campaign Fund Act basically argued that it was at least a beginning. During the short 1966 debates the author and principal sponsor of the measure, Senator Long of Louisiana, repeatedly recognized its shortcomings. He suggested that having it on the books would enable Congress to do something about the flow of money and interest in campaigns because, for the first time, an adequate alternative to private finance would be available. He said that there was plenty of time before the 1968 elections for Congress to regulate or ban private contributions and strengthen reporting.[76] Senator Long argued that resources freed by public funding of presidential campaigns would trickle down to Senate, House, and gubernatorial candidates, thus giving candidates not only more resources but a wider variety of sources.[77]

The opposition to the Presidential Campaign Fund Act seemed to split into two groups, one opposed to the principle of public finance and another, which included the leader of the fight to repeal the Fund act, Senator Gore, favoring a greater public role in political campaigns but with specific objections to the 1966 act.

They made several points during the debates.[78] The 1966 act was inadequate, they said, because there were no guidelines on how public money was to be used. Senator Gore argued that to establish the Presidential Campaign Fund without simultaneously establishing strict controls over the use of private money in campaigns was to give up the opportunity for serious reform. He feared that the public money would just add to the total spent on campaigns and that the abuses caused by private finance would continue unchecked.

There was also some opposition to the specific funding device established by the 1966 act—a tax check-off. Some Senators believed it was an unhealthy precedent to allow individual taxpayers to designate how their tax money should be spent. Rather, if the public was to pay for presidential campaigns, it should use regular Treasury financing.

When Senator Mansfield introduced the compromise that ended debate on the subject,[79] he argued that an important principle—public finance for presidential campaigns—had been confirmed. The Senate ordered the Finance Committee to produce a comprehensive public campaign finance proposal within six weeks. The committee produced a bill, but no action was taken in either house.

The proposal was much more comprehensive in its approach to regulating and financing of federal elections. It tried to remedy many of the weaknesses discovered in the 1966 act. The bill recommended by the Senate Finance Committee in November 1967 provided candidates for President and Senate (the committee assumed the House would add itself when it considered the bill) with an opportunity to choose either public or private finance for their campaigns.[80] If a major party candidate opted for public finance, he could accept no private contributions.

Presidential candidates of major parties (defined as more than 25 per cent of the vote) who chose public financing would be eligible for a grant equaling 20 cents times the number of votes cast for major party candidates in the last presidential election. Each minor party presidential candidate (defined as receiving between 5 per cent and 25 per cent of the votes) using public financing would be given 40 cents for each vote cast for his party's candidate in either the previous or current election, whichever provided the larger amount. Minor party candidates could spend private money to cover costs that exceeded their public subsidies.

The formula for determining the public subsidy for senatorial candidates was somewhat different. The amount a candidate could receive was to be based on the total number of votes cast in the state in one of three previous elections: the two preceding senatorial elections or the preceding presidential election, whichever was largest. Candidates would be paid 50 cents for each of the first 200,000 votes, 35 cents for each of the next 200,000, and 20 cents for each vote over 400,000.

Minor party candidates using the same elections as a base were to receive $1.00 for the first 100,000 votes their party's candidate received, 70 cents for each of the next 100,000, and 40 cents for each vote over 200,000. Payments would have ranged from a minimum of $100,000 for each major party candidate in Alaska, Delaware, Vermont, and Wyoming, to $1.5 million for each major party candidate in California and New York.[51]

In contrast with the 1966 act, the 1967 bill appropriated money directly from the Treasury to candidates of both major and minor parties. No prior action such as a tax check-off was needed by a taxpayer.

The Finance Committee made another major change in its 1967 recommendations. Payments would be made only to candidate committees. Political parties would be prohibited from receiving any of the public funds. The committee took this course to minimize "the effect of these provisions on the existing political structure and institutions." The committee added recommendations for a tax credit of 50 per cent on contributions up to $50 on individual returns in the hope of encouraging new voluntary contributions to political parties and state and local candidates.

Reporting requirements were toughened considerably. The Comptroller General was to audit all claims for public reimbursement, and criminal penalties were provided to prevent abuses. The bill passed the Senate but died in House committee.

Direct Subsidies and the Public Interest

The current pattern of political finance is being strained to the point where private sources may not be able to provide the money to conduct 435 House and 34 or 35 Senate contests every two years. In fact, supporters of public finance insist that active public support is needed now.

Public financing would alleviate many of the fears and suspicions now generated by large special interest contributions. But it would not remove them from the political system. So long as economic interests are affected by the actions of politicians, they will attempt to be represented. If they cannot get access through campaign contributions, they will try to get their views represented in some other way.

Political parties and election campaigns have been publicly subsidized in Puerto Rico since 1957, but the parties continue to raise and spend substantial private funds as well. Since 1964, principal political parties (defined as receiving more than 5 per cent of the vote at the last election) are given a basic yearly allowance of $75,000 each for their regular operations. During an election campaign, each party is given a basic campaign credit of $75,000 for general expenses and another $12,500 to transport voters to the polls. They are also entitled to a share of additional funds totaling one million dollars based on the straight party vote they received in 1964.[82] (West Germany also provides its parties with extensive public subsidies. And private contributions to elections are also permitted.)

The United States 1966 Presidential Campaign Fund Act also channeled the money through the parties. The 1967 Finance Committee proposal, however, called for payments directly to candidate committees. In its comments on the 1967 proposal, the Senate Finance Committee said that providing subsidies directly to candidates rather than to parties would have little effect on our existing political institutions. That assumption is open to serious question.

Candidates are already essentially free from party influence in the nominating process because they can challenge a party decision in a primary election. Giving direct subsidies to candidates to run their general election campaigns would tend to make them independent of party influence and responsibility during and after the election as well.

The influence and position of political parties have been eroding in the United States for over fifty years. Yet, for all their weaknesses, party committees still serve as conduits for substantial campaign funds and assistance to candidates. Party labels still serve as indicators of how a candidate will vote in Congress and how the Congress will be organized. Political parties also perform important functions between elections. They help recruit new people. They register voters. And, in opposition, they form a focus for surveillance and criticism of government policy. If subsidies were restricted to candidates alone, parties might have an increasingly difficult time raising the money they need to fulfill these nonelectoral functions. The net result might be a weaker political system.

The money spent during and between elections by parties fills important public needs. If all elections were competitive and strong parties existed in all areas of the country, much more money would need to be spent on politics.

Public subsidies probably would not eliminate spending differences among candidates. But they would make the differences less critical if candidates received enough to make every election a real contest.[83]

Indirect Public Subsidies—Television

Since 1967 no action has been taken in either house of Congress on any proposal for direct subsidies for campaign expenses. However, many members of Congress as well as increasing numbers of voters feel that something must be done to stop the rapid rise of campaign costs. Attention has focused on those rising campaign costs that Congress could actually affect without cash subsidies, the principal one being television.

The use and cost of television in congressional campaigns has risen sharply in recent years, and regulating the use of television channels falls within the jurisdiction of Congress. Current federal policy on television in politics is limited to the equal time provision and the fairness doctrine. Section 315—the equal time provision—of the Federal Communications Act provides that a station that gives one candidate time has to give all his opponents a comparable opportunity to appear. In 1959 the section was amended to exclude regular news coverage and regularly scheduled news interview programs.

The fairness doctrine holds that when a public policy position is advocated either by the station itself through an editorial or documentary or by a spokesman for a group using the station's facilities, the station has an obligation to give responsible spokesmen for the other side an opportunity to reply.

Candidates campaign on television in either program-length appearances or spot announcements of ten to sixty seconds. Reformers almost universally prefer such television formats as debates, question and answer periods, discussions, or films. Candidates prefer spots, because they believe that they can more often capture more voters with their political defenses down with a quick message than with longer and considerably more edifying programs. In 1964, 73 per cent of the station charges were for spots; in 1968 the share was about the same, but total TV campaign expenditures rose by about 70 per cent.[84]

As a rule spots cost much more comparatively than program time. In some parts of the country, the cost of eight or ten one-minute spots might equal the cost of one half-hour of program time. Shorter spots are comparatively even more expensive. Production costs for spot advertisements are also relatively higher. And while discounts are available to regular and large-scale advertisers, stations usually charge political advertisers their highest rate. (In response to recent criticism a few networks and stations now give political advertisers discounts.)

Harry Ashmore of the Center for the Study of Democratic Institutions has recommended that paid campaign advertising on television and in other media be banned. Ashmore and others who oppose paid television advertising say that candidates for public office are not soap and they therefore should not be marketed like soap. Ashmore advocates heavy use of television campaigning in longer formats.

Other proposals to make television cheaper and more accessible to candidates include asking stations to give more free program time, and requiring that advertising and program time be sold to candidates at sharply reduced rates.

Many broadcasters and some members of Congress favor a voluntary approach.[85] They argue that stations will respond to the public interest. Station owners have claimed that if the equal time provision were repealed, they would be free to give time available to major party congressional candidates without having to give equal time to every minor candidate. But the record of broadcasters in areas where congressional races had only two candidates has not been particularly good.[86] Thirty-four states had senatorial races in 1964 and twenty involved only two major party candidates. (Minor party candidates ran in the other fourteen states.) In both categories, the number of television stations that reported giving free time was the same, 29 per cent. In the eleven states that had close senatorial elections, 90 per cent of the television stations sold commercial time to the candidates but only 32 per cent gave them any free time.[87] And when they did, the time that was given was almost never prime time, when most voters are actually viewing.

Requiring stations to provide a fixed amount of free time to candidates for Congress or political parties, some in prime time, is a logical alternative. The purchase of additional commercial advertising time might or might not be banned. Besides, television campaigning is not suited to many congressional districts. The forty or so congressional districts in the New York prime viewing area create a real problem for any free time proposal. Would the eleven television stations in New York be forced to provide free time for all the New York and nearby New Jersey and Connecticut candidates? If they all took advantage of the free time, the stations point out, there would be little time for any other programming.

The most serious objection to all proposals for free program time is that they do not give candidates what they feel they need or, in fact, what they spend their own campaign money on—spot advertisements. Thus unless spots are actually prohibited, which is unlikely, the cost of campaigning would continue to rise and rich candidates or those with access to big money would continue to enjoy an advantage over poorer ones.

A bill recently passed by the Senate would reduce the prices stations can charge candidates for federal office for air time. It also places a ceiling on the amount of time a candidate can buy. This bill faces stiff opposition in the House and from the Nixon administration before it can become law.

Another new proposal would require lower rates for all commercial time purchases and allow broadcasters to deduct as business expenses the revenues lost in the discounts.[88] In this way the public would share the expense of television campaign advertising by giving broadcasters a tax break.

Most broadcasters oppose requirements to set aside time or sell it at a fixed discount. They argue that mandating reduced-price prime time during the five-week period prior to an election would interfere with their normal fall programming schedule and cause them serious losses for the whole year. Moreover, they feel that prime time interruptions for political programs would annoy viewers, particularly in areas serving several House districts. Some broadcasters have complained that such proposals are unconstitutional invasions of their rights.

Supporters of these proposals contend that where television is appropriate for congressional campaigning—usually outside the major metropolitan areas—it would bring the cost down to what the average candidate could afford. They do not believe it would encourage use of television by candidates who do not use it now—those in large metropolitan areas—because even at reduced rates, the return for candidates in these areas would still be very low.

Free or Reduced Television Rates and the Public Interest

Guaranteed access to television exposure for all candidates might well contribute to creating more competitive elections. When it is properly used, television can help a candidate overcome recognition problems quickly. But reducing the price of television advertising is not the same as making it available to all candidates. Even at 20 to 30 per cent of the regular price, television can be very expensive, especially when production costs are added. A prime time one-minute spot might well cost, even at the reduced rate, $500, and a professionally produced announcement to fill it might cost several thousand dollars.

Requiring candidates to appear, as one recent report suggested, might produce informative and responsible campaigning. But what about those political candidates who do not perform well on television? A campaign finance system that helps candidates communicate in only one way might create unfair advantages.

Even though television is a very powerful medium, guaranteeing candidates for Congress access to it will not solve all the problems. Congress might also consider use of other campaign communications it controls, such as free postage, free or cheap access to radio, and reduced magazine and newspaper advertising rates. In these ways, candidates who do not want to use television still will have augmented access to voters.

V. Redistributing Political Costs

It might be easier for candidates to find enough money for the political costs of their campaigns, if the nonpartisan costs of campaigns were paid for from other sources. The United States is the only industrial democracy in which the government does not pay the costs of keeping eligible voters registered. Candidates and political organizations do. If the state or federal governments assumed responsibility for registering voters, additional party and candidate resources would be available to wage competitive political campaigns. Much money is also spent by candidates on election day getting voters to the polls. In many congressional campaigns, over 20 per cent of the budget goes for election day activities. Other election day costs, such as child care and transportation, could also be shifted away from the campaign treasuries.

If Congress is willing to give people a tax credit for making a cash contribution, it might be even more productive to give them a tax credit for the real costs of participating in the election. A modest tax credit issued at the polls might make it possible for more people to vote, at less cost to the candidate.

Expensive mistakes are made in political campaigns because just about the only training available is on-the-job. Almost half the congressional campaigns every two years are run by people who have never run one before. In recent years professional firms have moved in to supply campaign management and training. Even though they are increasing rapidly, there will probably never be enough of these firms to run all the competitive elections that take place. And their fees add to campaign costs of political parties and candidates. The people who pay the bills have become more acutely aware of this problem in recent years as demands for political funds mount. They are now concerned about proper training of campaign managers. This concern, however, has not yet produced much good training. Parties alone probably cannot do the job of political training that is really required since many of their leaders are poorly trained.

In short, if limited campaign resources are to be used well, a lot of people will need training. The parties, universities, and other institutions with training skills should share that task. They should train party workers, campaign managers, and fund raisers.

Examining campaign practices to remove those that properly belong in other parts of the political system is a useful approach. It may eventually reverse the essentially negative traditional view of politics. It recognizes that the political system has legitimate needs and looks for an adequate way to fill them.

The current system does not provide enough money where it is needed to produce genuinely competitive campaigns. It is contributing to a rigidity and sterility in the Congress at a time that demands flexibility and new blood.

APPENDIX

Federal Corrupt Practices Act and Recent Proposals: A Comparison

	FEDERAL CORRUPT PRACTICES ACT 2 U.S. Code, 241-256 18 U.S. Code, 591-613	ASHMORE-GOODELL BILL (HR 11233) 1968	ELECTION REFORM ACT OF 1967 (S. 1880)
Definitions: *Election:*	General or special; not primary or convention.	General, special, or primary; party convention or caucus; primary to select delegates to national nominating convention; presidential nominating primary.	Same as HR 11233.
Candidate:	Individual whose name is presented for election. (302)	One who seeks nomination to federal office and is shown to be seeking nomination by (1) taking action under state law to qualify himself for nomination or (2) receiving contributions or making expenditures or giving consent for another person to do same, for purposes of campaign.	Same as HR 11233.
Political committee:	Group which accepts contributions or makes expenditures to influence elections of candidates or electors, (1) in 2 or more states or (2) whether or not in more than 1 state if such group is a branch of a national committee, association, or organization.	Any individual or group which accepts contributions or makes expenditures in an aggregate amount exceeding $1,000 in one year. (591) Exception: committees which primarily support state and local cands. and operate in one state only.	Any individual or group which accepts contributions or makes expenditures in an aggregate amount exceeding $1,000 in 1 year.
Contribution:	Gift, subscription, loan, advance, or deposit, of money, or anything of value, and includes a contract, promise, or agreement to make a contribution.	Gift, donation, loan (except from licensed loan inst.) etc., and includes contract, promise, etc. to make a contribution, and includes transfer of funds between political committees.	Same as HR 11233.

Expenditure:	Payment, contribution, loan, etc. and includes a contract, promise, etc. to make an expenditure.	Purchase, payment, distribution, etc. and includes a contract, etc. to make an expenditure, and includes a transfer of funds between political committees.	Same as HR 11233.
Reports: *Who makes reports and to whom:*	Treasurers of political committees file with Clerk of House. House candidates file with Clerk of House. Senate candidates file with Secretary of Senate. Individuals contributing $50 or more, not through a committee, file with Clerk.	Repository of reports is 5-man, bipartisan Federal Elections Commission apptd. by President for 10-yr. terms. Copy of each report must be filed with Clerk of U.S. District Court in which committee or candidate is headquartered. Political committees spending or receiving $1,000 or more in 1 year; candidates; and persons contributing or spending more than $100 not through committee; must all file reports.	Political committees and House candidates file with Clerk of House. Political committees and candidates for Senate, President, and Vice President file with Secretary of Senate. Individuals contributing $100 or more or spending $100 or more not through committees must file. All political committees spending or receiving $1,000 or more in 1 year must file report. Must file also with U.S. District Court.
Content of reports:	Itemized account of contributions and expenditures. Names and address of contributors of $100 or more. Personal expenses (travel, personal, postage, printing, telephone, circulars, etc.) of candidates do not have to be itemized; total must be reported. Total from other contributors (less than $100 each). Statement of every promise made in regard to appointment to public or private office.	List of contributors of $100 or more (including purchasers of tickets to fund-raising events). Total from other contributors. List of candidates and political committees making or receiving transfers of funds. List of loans of $100 or more except from licensed loan companies. Total of proceeds from fund-raising events and campaign paraphernalia. Total of all receipts. List of persons receiving expends. of $100 or more, and purpose of expenditure. List of persons receiving expenditures for personal services and salaries of $100 or more. Total of expenditures. Amount of debts owed by or to committee.	Same as HR 11233 excluding provisions on loans from licensed loan companies.

(continued on following page)

	FEDERAL CORRUPT PRACTICES ACT 2 U.S. Code, 241-256 18 U.S. Code, 591-613	ASHMORE-GOODELL BILL (HR 11233) 1968	ELECTION REFORM ACT OF 1967 (S. 1880)
Filing dates:	Committees: between 1st and 10th of March, June, and Sept. each year; btn. 10th and 15th, and on 5th day preceding general election; and on Jan. 1st for preceding year. Candidates: btn. 10 and 15 days before, and within 30 days after, general election.	10th of March, June and Sept., 15th and 5th days preceding elections, and by Jan. 31. Convention committees must file financial report within 60 days after convention, not later than 20 days before elector selection.	Same as HR 11233. Same as HR 11233.
Other accounting requirements for political committees:	Must keep itemized accounts of contributions and expenditures, with name and address and date. Must keep receipted bill of each expenditure over $10. All contributions made to committee must be reported to treasurer.	Must have receipted bills for all expenditures over $100 and for lesser expends. if total in one year to same person is more than $100. All contributions must be reported to treasurer of committee.	Same as HR 11233.
Public Inspection:	Reports must be open to public inspection.	Commission must: Make reports available for public inspection and copying. Publish annual report. Make audits and field investigations if indicated. Report violations to law enforcement officials.	Duties for Clerk and Secretary are same as for Commission.
Penalties:		Penalties of fines and/or imprisonment for violations.	Same as HR 11233.
Gifts and Honorariums:		Senators and Representatives must file every Jan. 31 a statement listing gifts received by him or spouse or children. Name and address of donors of $100 must be reported. Honorariums exceeding $100 must be reported	

Effect on State Laws:		State laws are not affected by provisions of this bill.
Registration:	Political committees must register with Commission if will make or spend $1,000 or more in 1 year.	Same as HR 11233, except that registration occurs with Clerk and Secretary.
Use of Funds for Personal Purposes:	Contributions to campaigns may not be used by candidates for personal purposes. Penalty: fine or imprisonment.	
Limits on Expenditures by Candidates: 1. $10,000 for Senate; $2,500 for Represent. 2. or: 3¢ times votes cast for all candidates for that office in preceding election, not to exceed $25,000 for Sen., or $5,000 for Rep. 3. Exempt from limitation: Personal, traveling, subsistence, stationery, postage, circulars, posters, telephone.		Repealed.
Limits on Committee Expenditures: $3 million.	Repealed.	Repealed.
Prohibitions on Contributors: 1. Soliciting U.S. employees for contributions prohibited. 2. Corporations, labor unions, natl. banks prohibited from making contributions to federal campaigns. 3. Federal contractors prohibited from making contributions to any campaign.	Same.	Same.
Limits on Individual Contributions: $5,000 per individual.	$5,000 in *aggregate* to all committees for same candidate.	Same as HR 11233.

Notes to Background Paper

1. The congressional franking privilege is in theory restricted to nonpolitical uses. Since 1968, however, the Post Office Department has given up trying to enforce the restriction.

2. Message of the President to Congress dated May 26, 1966, transmitting the President's proposals for election reform.

3. For excellent recent examinations of political finance see Alexander Heard, *The Costs of Democracy,* University of North Carolina Press, Chapel Hill, 1960; and David Adamany, *Financing Politics, Recent Wisconsin Elections,* University of Wisconsin Press, Madison, 1969. The Adamany book is an extremely thorough examination of state-level political finance.

4. Ray Wolfinger and Joan Heifitz, "Safe Seats, Seniority and Power in Congress," *American Political Science Review,* June 1965, pp. 337-349.

5. For an excellent discussion of the politics of reapportionment see Robert B. McKay, *Reapportionment: The Law and Politics of Equal Representation,* The Twentieth Century Fund, New York, 1965.

6. Article I, Section 4 of the Constitution.

7. 5 U.S. Code, 1964 edition, Paragraph 118.

8. 5 U.S. Code, 1964 edition, 1502-1506, and Civil Service Rules and Regulations, part I, chapter III. (Civil Service Pamphlet #20.)

9. See Herbert Croly, *Marcus Alonzo Hanna,* Shoe String Press, Inc., Hampton, Conn., p. 325.

10. See Perry Belmont, *An American Democrat,* A.M.S. Press, New York, 1941.

11. 18 U.S. Code, 1964 edition, 591-613.

12. Heard, *op. cit.,* p. 211.

13. Now part of U.S. Code, 610.

14. Commission of Party Structure and Delegate Selection, Democratic National Committee, "A Profile of State Public Disclosure Laws" (mimeo), November 1969.

15. It is a common practice for special interest lobbyists to buy many tickets to $100 fund-raising testimonial dinners. Most of these contributions go unreported because ticket purchasers can remain anonymous.

16. More than ten such indictments against public relations firms and corporations were issued in 1969. Two shipping firms were fined $50,000 each for illegal political contributions early in 1970.

17. Adamany, *op. cit.,* pp. 180-181.

18. 18 U.S. Code, 1964 edition, 248.

19. See U.S. Senate, 89th Congress, Second Session, *Election Law Guidebook,* Document 91, 1966. Table X, Election Offenses, p. 164.

20. New York *Times,* July 9, 1969.

21. 2 U.S. Code, 1964 edition, 244.

22. 2 U.S. Code, 1964 edition, 246.

23. 2 U.S. Code, 1964 edition, 241.

24. 2 U.S. Code, 1964 edition, 245.

25. Estimate drawn from private discussions with Herbert E. Alexander and others.

26. Reports filed included primary and general election spending for Max Rafferty, Thomas Kuchel, and Alan Cranston.

27. *Congressional Quarterly,* Vol. XXVII, No. 49, December 5, 1969, p. 2435.

28. *Ibid.,* pp. 2445-2456.

29. For example, Abraham Ribicoff reported personal expenditures of $5,000 at the federal level and nothing for committee expenditures. According to the report he filed after the election with the Connecticut Secretary of State, he spent $586,068. From Hartford *Courant,* December 6, 1968.

30. 2 U.S. Code, 1964 edition, 247.

31. Political committee and House reports go to the Clerk of the House; Senate reports go to the Secretary of the Senate.

32. Louise Overacker, *Money and Politics,* Macmillan, New York, 1932.

33. See for example, Donald R. Matthews, *U.S. Senators and Their World,* Vintage, New York, 1960; and William S. White, *The Citadel: The Story of the U.S. Senate,* Harper, New York, 1956.

34. New York *Post,* October 10, 1969.

35. New York *Times,* February 8, 1970.

36. New York *Times,* January 29, 1970.

37. For a more comprehensive review of state reporting regulations see Laura Denny and Herbert Alexander, *Regulation of Political Finance,* University of California, Institute of Government, Berkeley, 1966.

38. For a more comprehensive review of the Florida experience see Elston Roady, "Ten Years of Florida's 'Who Gave It—Who Got It' Law," *Law and Contemporary Problems,* 27, Summer 1962, pp. 434-446. The bulk of the data included in this section is drawn from the Roady article.

39. *Congress and the Nation,* Vol. II, Congressional Quarterly, Washington, D.C., 1969, p. 645.

40. See for example Murray Levin, *Kennedy Campaigning,* Beacon Press, Boston, 1966.

41. Story by Martha Angle in the Washington *Evening Star,* September 22, 1969.

42. *Ibid.*

43. *Congress and the Nation,* Vol. II, Congressional Quarterly, Washington, D.C., 1969, pp. 443-446 is the source of data for this brief review.

44. 86th Congress, Second Session. S. 2436 passed the Senate on January 25, 1960, by a vote of 59–22 (Democrats 38–15, Republicans 21–7).

45. 87th Congress, First Session. S. 2426 passed the Senate on September 15, 1961, by voice vote.

46. President's Commission on Campaign Costs, *Financing Presidential Campaigns,* Government Printing Office, Washington, D.C., April 1962, p. 5.

47. The Presidential Transition Act of 1963, PL-88-277.

48. State of the Union Message, January 12, 1966.

49. Message of the President on financing federal elections, May 26, 1966.

50. 90th Congress, First Session, "Election Reform Act of 1967," Senate Report 515, Report of the Committee on Rules and Administration to accompany S. 1880, Government Printing Office, Washington, D.C., August 16, 1967, p. 2.

51. *Ibid.,* part 2.

52. 90th Congress, Second Session, "Election Reform Act of 1968," House Report No. 1593, Government Printing Office, Washington, D.C., June 27, 1968.

53. *Congress and the Nation,* Vol. II, Congressional Quarterly, Washington, D.C., 1969, p. 446.

54. Surveys taken by both Gallup and the Survey Research Center over the last twenty years confirm this figure.

55. Survey Research Center, University of Michigan, postelection poll, 1968.

56. Twentieth Century Fund Commission on Campaign Costs in the Electronic Era, *Voters' Time,* The Twentieth Century Fund, New York, 1969.

57. For a comprehensive review of this experiment see Alexander Heard (ed.), *Bipartisan Political Fund Raising: Two Experiments in 1964,* Citizens' Research Foundation, Princeton, N.J., 1967.

58. *Ibid.*

59. Interview with Vincent Barabba, President of Decision Making Information, Inc., in Los Angeles, May 15, 1969.

60. Interview with executive secretary of the Montgomery County Democratic Committee, February 26, 1970.

61. Interview with Kent Wold, Effective Citizens Organization, Washington, D.C., February 26, 1970.

62. Interview with James Hurt, Manager of Civic Affairs, Hughes Aircraft Corporation, Los Angeles, February 1970.

63. Wold interview.

64. Interview with Mary Zon, March 6, 1970.

65. President's Commission, 1962, pp. 13-17.

66. California, Hawaii, Missouri, Minnesota, Oklahoma.

67. Interview with Allan N. Desin, Research Analyst, California State Franchise Tax, Sacramento, February 21, 1970.

68. *Ibid.*

69. See for example Adamany, pp. 256-262.

70. Senator Long, a vocal defender of the oil depletion allowance, has often said, "If I didn't represent oil I wouldn't represent Louisiana."

71. 89th Congress, Second Session, "Financing Political Campaigns," Senate Hearings before the Committee on Finance, August 18 and 19, 1966, Government Printing Office, Washington, D.C., p. 78.

72. The act provided major parties with equal shares of $1.00 per major party voter in the previous presidential election.

73. The repeal was debated on the Senate floor as an amendment to the Foreign Investors Tax Act (HR 13103) from April 3, 1967, through May 9, 1967.

74. *Congressional Quarterly Almanac* for 1967, Washington, D.C., 1968.

75. *Ibid.*, p. 295.

76. 89th Congress, Second Session, *Congressional Record*, p. 26384.

77. 90th Congress, First Session, *Congressional Record,* April 3, 1967, statement by Senator Long of Louisiana.

78. *Ibid.*, statements by Senator Gore, Senator Williams, and Senator James B. Pearson of Kansas.

79. May 9, 1967.

80. 90th Congress, First Session, "Honest Elections Act of 1967," Senate Report 714, Government Printing Office, Washington, D.C.

81. *Ibid.*, p. 20.

82. For a comprehensive review of the Puerto Rican experience see Henry Wells, *Government Financing of Political Parties in Puerto Rico,* Citizens' Research Foundation, Princeton, 1961; and Henry Wells and Robert Anderson, *Government Financing of Political Parties in Puerto Rico: A Supplement to Study Number Four,* Citizens' Research Foundation, Princeton, 1966.

83. See Adamany, pp. 256-262.

84. Federal Communications Commission, "Survey of Political Broadcasting, Primary and General Election," Washington, D.C., August 1969.

85. See 91st Congress, First Session, *The Campaign Broadcast Reform Act of 1969,* Senate Hearings, October 21-23, 1969, *passim.*

86. See Herbert Alexander, Stimson Bullitt, and Hyman Goldin, "The High Cost of T.V. Campaigns," *Television Quarterly,* Winter 1966, pp. 47-65.

87. *Ibid.*, p. 62.

88. *Voters' Time.*